The Untold SECRET that Creates True Wealth

Discover how business legends achieve their ultimate treasure.

By Brig Hart and John Beehner

Other books by Brig Hart

Why not you, Why not now: the Brig Hart story

Hope for Economic Homeless, your hand up no hand out

Ultimate Success God's Way

Other Books by John F. Beehner

True Wealth By the Book

The Freedom Revolution...Rocking our World

By The Book Publishing

3721 San Jose Place, Suite 1

Jacksonville, FL 32257

www.AskWiseCounsel.com

www.USAAssoc.com

ISBN-13: 978-1494708344   ISBN-10: 1494708345

The Untold Secret...What others are saying...

"I deal with many wealthy executives who wish they had known the Secret passage Brig and John uncovered in this fascinating book. It would have saved them many frustrations and inspired them."

BILL GLYNN, CEO BRAND EQUITY, LLC., A PRIVATE EQUITY HOLDING COMPANY

"I have loaned money to hundreds of companies , so I know the 'Untold Secret' can help any entrepreneur and lender see the obstacles and joy in pursuing their True Wealth. It's a must read I recommend it to all my clients. "

BENNETT BROWN, CEO OF AMERICAN ENTERPRISE BANK

"This amazing book and its stories will give the eternal wisdom that you need to put your success journey into perspective and give you the peace of mind that you are not alone."

CARTER LE CRAW, FOUNDER AMERICAN VALUES INVESTMENT GROUP

"The Untold Secret is one of the most inspiring books I've ever read. I wish I had read it when I was much younger. I would encourage everyone of my franchisees to read it to give them the wisdom that encourage them to persevere."

PAUL DAVIS, FOUNDER, PAUL DAVIS RESTORATION SYSTEMS, INT.

"I have served in the corporate world and helped small businesses grow. So when I previewed "the Untold Secret," I could quickly see where Brig and John have cracked the code for Ultimate Success. Making money is good and necessary but it's about visions and perseverance that produces True Wealth."

JIM DISMORE, FOUNDER OF KINGDOM WAY
AND ORIGINAL VP OF MARKETING FOR SAM WALTON AT WAL-MART

Table of Contents

The Untold Secret ... reveals the *patterns, obstacles and cycles* our Creator incorporated for Entrepreneurs and leaders *that will test and challenge their Character, Humility, Obedience and Persistence and lead them to their True Wealth.*

Overview

Can you obtain the same level of wealth as Donald Trump, Warren Buffet, Steve Jobs or Bill Gates with their super-rich accomplishments? Hundreds of authors and millionaires have attempted to explain their formula so that you can duplicate their super success. But can you believe them?

True Wealth is not inherited but created through visions, dreams, hard work, ups and downs, failures and successes—it is far more than riches, money or possessions. It encompasses the deeper things of life that affect your body, soul and spirit and accomplishments in life.

Authors and entrepreneurs Brig Hart and John Beehner ask, *"Did three men in different writings in the first century AD record a 'secret' for all mankind?"* They contend you will never hear or learn about this on celebrity shows. On their life quests Brig and John have worked coached or inspired hundreds of entrepreneurs to discover the fastest road to make their first $10 million. Ultimately, the real truth behind creating wealth evades most people, but is rooted in the trials and tests that leaders experience in life and business.

The depth and richness of this book lies in the stories of entrepreneurs that have built their companies like Nike, McDonalds, IBM, Mary Kay, Apple, Microsoft, Facebook, J.C. Penney, Starbucks, Quaker Oats, MonaVie, Southwest Airlines, Jet Blue, CNN, FedEx just to name just a few. It is the powerful inside example of 'sowing and reaping' that the media fails to share with its audiences. They still believe 'bad news outsells the good News' and profound insight of this book, "The Untold Secret" unlocks the mystery behind successful men and women who have received a vision and mission. See how they produced a harvest in difficult soil and inspire their staff with their passionate spirit.

In today's marketplace, the word 'secret' is widely used by marketers, but Brig and John discovered the foundational truth that Jesus taught over 2,000 years ago. He seldom used the word 'secret' so when He used the word you have to listen intently. Three times in Matthew, Luke, and Mark, the "Secret of the Kingdom" is presented by Jesus as found in the Parable of the Sower. The parable describes what happens when the seed is sown on hard soil, rocky soil, thorny soil, and good soil.

If you are called to be a passionate risk taker in life or business, this book will inspire you with faith, hope, and encouragement. By uncovering untold truths, you can make sense out of your calling in a journey filled with successes, potholes, confusion and unanswered questions. Discover what God can do and is doing through you as the gardener of your soul. Be prepared to change. The achievements of life are found in the soil of your soul. Don't miss the opportunity to find your path to ultimate treasures.

A Fundamental Cornerstone for this book

John Beehner tells the story of the perspective he and Brig hope most readers will gain that can inspire their life and journey toward achieving True wealth.

In 1964, my wife Judy and I set out on a great adventure after just 30 days of marriage. We joined the Peace Corps while the words of President John F. Kennedy were still ringing in our ears "Ask not what your country can do for you, but what you can do for your country." We began our journey to Brazil at Arizona State University for three months of training in Tempe, Arizona.

Little did we know that of the nearly 100 people selected for the Brazilian assignment over half would be "selected out" because of more testing, reference checks and counseling.

The three months of trainer were vigorous. Portuguese training six hours a day, field projects, lectures and so much more. During this training, one professor from ASU who was teaching on the Brazilian culture said something profound that still impacts my thinking today. In fact I believe it's the real purpose of this book. He said, "You will get down to your city and get orientated the first month and 'Culture Shock' will set in. You will say to yourself, 'Oh my gosh, how did we get here, what are we doing here? This is hard, I really don't understand the language and maybe I should go home?' Some of you will leave, but most will say, 'We can't do that, we made a commitment.' But the 'Culture Shock' phenomenon continues and within the next three months you will say the same thing. Then again, at six months, nine months and then at a year you will repeat your frustration. But at a year you will say something different—you will say, 'Oh, its okay, we have made it this far, we can make it another year.'" (At the time Peace Corps assignments were normally for two years).

That statement was true for Judy and me. Every time we said, "this is not working, maybe we should go home?" We always pointed back to the words of the professor—"You will have days like this." Okay, he was right, let's just hang in there and do our best.

That story is symbolic. The purpose of this book is to tell there is divine purpose in your journey on this earth. There will be testing all along on your journey to pursue your calling and purpose in life, business or ministry. We will tell you the roadblocks, patterns and cycles of up and downs and how others have journeyed before you.

And there is True Wealth at the end of your journey.

Dedication

by John Beehner

The late Charles 'Red' Scott was born and raised in Paris, Texas in the 1920's into a poor family. After Red graduated as President of his High School Senior class he worked as a writer for the local newspaper. Yet, in a surprising way he discovered he was eligible for a scholarship to the University of Texas. He worked his way through school and received a Journalism degree. While working for the Dallas Morning Star he felt discontent, so he joined an investment-banking firm, which he and his partners later leveraged into a significant business. Then one day he was lured to La Jolla, California to take over a hemorrhaging business. He had the opportunity to turnaround for their investors. That experience opened the door for him to acquire more businesses, which grew into a public conglomerate of twelve companies. This group was called Intermark. During a twelve year run, his multiple companies grew a compounded pace of over 40% a year.

Yet, Red was different from the other high flying CEOs of public companies. He stood only 5'9" and spoke with a Texas drawl and instantly achieved respect and admiration with his peers because of his *"real and humble"* personality and charm. It was not long before he became a member and even President of the Horatio Alger Association of Distinguished American (mostly CEOs with rags to riches stories of success).

Red went out of his way while leading his $2 billion company to speak to the entrepreneurs in my business five times a year and always impacted their thinking with profound wisdom, humor and street smarts. In 1995, John was blessed to sell his growing business called TEC Florida (now Vistage) to him since he wanted to retire from running large companies. He was 'a man of character' who every entrepreneur admired. He and John's former staff more than doubled the TEC business in a few short years.

Here's just a slice of the things he shared with CEOs.

Charles 'Red' Scott and his Legacy

The quality of one's life absolutely depends upon the degree to which we align ourselves with and feel a sense of Reverence for God— Our Creator and Father. Service is the virtue that distinguishes the one grade of all times by which we will be remembered. It places a mark of nobility upon its disciples. It is the dividing line, which separates the people groups of the world:

- *Those who help or those who hinder*

- *Those who lift or those who lean*

- *Those who contribute or those who consume*

How much better it is to give than to receive! Service in any form is both generous and beautiful. To just give encouragement, to impart sympathy, to show interest, to banish fear, to build self confidence, or simply to awaken some hope in the hearts of others ... NO GREATER SERVICE OR GIFT CAN ONE GIVE!

This book is dedicated to Red's kindness, example and character and many men and women like him (many of whom are mentioned in this book) that have influenced Brig and I...and some many others with their great leadership.

Defining True Wealth

by Brig Hart

3 John 2 *Beloved, "I wish above all things*
that you may prosper and be in health,
even as your soul prospers." (KJV)

Wealth by the media's or world's terms, normally reflects the strength of your personal assets or balance sheet. There is nothing wrong with making and accumulating assets, money or even toys. I've been rich, and I've been poor....rich is better. But as a Believer in my Creator, I am Wealthy because of who He is and what He has done through my life. I was lost and had no concept of how to be strong or make money in my youth. Thank God He saved me from my ignorance and immaturity through His loving Grace and Sacrifice for me. No amount of wealth in this world compares to the changes He lead me to...to transform my life and thinking.

Acquiring wealth comes by recognizing the seed visions He sends our way and then simply living by the law of sowing and reaping. You have to give your heart or even possessions to others, before you will receive in return. God's plan is all about faithfulness, diligence and obedience in what He wants from your life. There are Character traits and principles that must be incorporated in your life in order to tap into true and sustaining wealth. Give and it shall be given unto you. God is all about Stewardship vs. Selfish gain or how much one can accumulate.

My advice for succeeding and becoming wealthy is to do the best you can with what you have, right now, and don't complain about what you don't have. God will make up the deficiencies. Keep your focus toward serving others. Wealthy is what I am because of Christ in my life... Wealthy is what I have become as a result of the sweat equity I have invested seeking His visions and using my gifts and talents. If I market an excellent product or service, at as good or better price to my targeted customers, we will win together. Doing that consistently well over time, and then stewarding what I received in return properly adds up quickly. I am Rich because of who I am and Wealthy because of how I have managed the substance given to me in the process.

Where your heart is, there will your treasure be also. See everything in light of eternity... store up for yourself, treasures in heaven because you can't take anything with you except the influence of Christ you have had on others.

God put in the heart of every man, woman and child the desire to find true wealth. So get your Mind, Will and Emotions in order and the results can and will bring the prosperity that can develop into Wealth when done with the right motive and intent.

CHAPTER 1

The American Dream of Success

Recently, John spoke with 15 people who have immigrated in the last few years to the United States from countries like the Ukraine, Russia, Iraq,, Bosnia, South Africa and China. Why did they come? And why do others keep coming? They claim it has been hard, but they love it here. Yes, despite the propaganda of the bitter and jealous, there is an enduring world image that America is still the land of opportunity.

One said, *"my worst day in America is better than my best day in my mother country."* As Americans, most of us believe this.

However, the question remains, why do they keep coming? A bad economy in America is still better than 95% of the other nations in the world. They come for freedom and opportunity to live a better life. Many come and earn enough money to send home a major portion to help their family or save until they can get them here. Others come because they want a piece of the American Dream—they want to be millionaires.

Is there a secret to why over half the billionaires in the world are Americans? Yet, we have only 5% of the world's population.

After 30 years of working with hundreds of entrepreneurs that have made over a million dollars (most multi-millionaires), we have discovered the secret. YES, there is a secret. But we have never read a business or motivational book—and we have researched hundreds—or met an entrepreneur who could really share the truth that you will discover in this writing.

Instead, we both discovered this secret and watched it change lives. How did we discover the secret? It's been divinely inspired as well as confirmed by reading and studying the number one selling book of all time. But before we go much further, allow us to share the answer from a backdrop of the two different mindsets that exist in our society.

The first story illustrates the perceptions and thoughts of many Americans. It is a story about Ted Turner, (founder and pioneer of CNN, Turner Broadcasting, Atlanta Braves and many other businesses). However, you can easily substitute Ted's name for so many other successful entrepreneurs that have achieved a high level of business success.

Ted's American Dream

It wasn't too many years ago that Ted sold off the majority of his business, CNN and Turner Broadcasting. After merging with Time Warner and AOL, he said to his wife at the time, Jane Fonda, *"I'm exhausted and we have got to get away for a while."*

She had heard that a romantic coastal town in Costa Rica was a wonderful getaway and they decided to go. While there, they happened to meet a young Costa Rican man by the name of Pedro, who took executives on fishing trips. One day, out on the water with Pedro, something miraculous happened. They caught 35 fish in one trip!

Pedro fascinated Ted, and he said, *"Pedro, what did you do? Did you put something special on the bait that we used? What is your secret?"*

Pedro answered, *"I have secret lures that I've developed over the* years. *I have seven of them that work practically every time, depending upon the waters, and I know just what to use at the right time of day."*

Ted was so impressed and fascinated by the whole experience that he said, *"You may have a great business opportunity here. You could do very well with this and you might even become a millionaire. I'm sure you'd be able to grow outside this area!"*

Pedro looked confused, *"I don't understand this, Senor ?"*

Ted tried to explain, *"Don't you see? You'd be able to manufacture these lures by the thousands. You could do so well that you'd be able to have a better lifestyle. I could help you with some capital, and we'd be able to get you a plant in the United States, maybe two or three."*

Pedro told Ted, *"I still don't understand. Why?"*

Ted tried to break it down even further, *"When you get to the United States, the lifestyle is so much better. There is so much you could do. You'd be very wealthy. Pretty soon, your company could go public, and you'd have many people working for you and lots of money. You would have an incredibly successful business. The reporters will want to interview you and find out your secret to success. You will become famous."*

Pedro replied, *"But I still don't understand why. Maybe I don't understand your American lingo."*

Ted continued, *"Well, after you do all these things you could sell the business, have a lot of money and possessions, and retire anywhere in the world, even to a small fishing village like this."*

Then Pedro said, *"Ah. Now I understand, but I think I will just stay and keep my simple lifestyle . . . in this small fishing village. Muches as gracias."*

Ted was referring to the 'American Dream,' the 'Rags to Riches Story,' or the 'Self Made Man' mindset. Stories of having very little, but making it big!

The question is: Is this hype or truth? Fact or fiction?

Can anyone be successful like Ted Turner?

So, what is the REAL SECRET?

The World's View:
Success is Based on Performance

Ted's thinking is the norm for most Americans. Many who have a hunger for leadership and 'making their mark' pursue success based on this perspective of our society. This is mostly media driven through news coverage, movies, TV portrayals, and especially books.

In the early part of our lives, that is also what we sought—worldly success. We wanted to satisfy our inner desire to 'be somebody.' In fact, we wanted a great deal out of life and were going for it. John vividly remembers the years when he was attempting to climb the corporate ladder, but in his heart, he wanted to have his own business. Whenever his family went to the mall, his wife took the kids shopping while he searched the bookstores. Like Brig he scoured the aisles, looking for the success magazines and books on starting your own business. We both wanted to determine the difference between successful people and those that don't make the cut.

For our purposes, let's start with defining what success is and look at the two different models. The first is the 'World's Perspective.' It is what we call the public persona or the person-on-the-street opinion. It's what we hear from other people, friends, and neighbors and it's what the media feeds us through movies, newspapers, advertising, music, and TV portrayals. Others tell us about right and wrong, good and bad, and success and failure.

Everyone agrees that since the 1950s, America's values and ethics have shifted. We are given the impression being successful in life is all about making it BIG. We are supposed to acquire great wealth, become famous, and have lots of possessions as well as personal power to control people or things. That is really what Ted Turner was trying to tell Pedro in our story. In fact, he just assumed that Pedro would get it. So, is our impression of the American Dream true—or only partially true?

Based on the popular world view, the traits for success involve:

- Accumulating money and wealth

- Finding fame or notoriety

- Accumulating possessions

- Having and using power

Money & Wealth

Money makes the world go 'round'—or so that is what we're told. The world's first attribute for being successful is money, riches, or wealth. If you are not a millionaire or at least earning $200,000 plus a year you're not successful—it used to be only $100,000, but inflation has taken over. Isn't that the perception we're fed all the time?

Search Amazon.com, and you'll find there are more than 70,000 books with the word millionaire, rich, or wealthy in their titles. That is a testimony to the American perception that with enough money, you can buy your way to happiness.

The historical trend in America is to use money to lure us. We fall for moneymaking schemes that involve reselling products, knowledge, or programs. They entice us with their fantastic formula for acquiring wealth.

Show Me the Money

In the movie Jerry Maguire, Tom Cruise plays the recently terminated sports agent struggling to build back his reputation while
Cuba Gooding, Jr. plays the professional football player hoping to
get a bigger contract. The classic and humorous line in the movie is,
"Show me the money."

That's the bottom line isn't it—the money. Wall Street, investment
groups, bankers, and the media want to get to that bottom line. In
fact, we can't prove our worth if we don't show them the money.
With many people, it begins to consume their thinking as they fer-
vently look out for #1 in greed.

Recently, John spent time with a CEO of a very successful company
that generously shared a high percentage of his profits with his staff.
And now, some of his staff are coming to him asking for a raise. It is
what some people call 'entitlement thinking.' That kind self-thinking
can discourage the entrepreneurs from sharing the greater rewards.

Millionaire Makeover

Laura Langmire, author and consultant, has written two different
books for wannabe millionaires. One is called the Millionaire Make-
over. She claims to have helped 400 people become millionaires.
She also claims that she can document her successful record of accomplishment. Having personally heard her speak, she is practical
and makes a lot of good sense. But is there credence to her claims?

Mark Victor Hansen, co-author of Chicken Soup for the Soul, has
authored the Automatic Wealth System, and now has a new book
titled, The One Minute Millionaire. A millionaire in a minute? Now,
that's something everyone wants!

You've seen these kinds of titles, not just in the bookstores but also
in magazine articles on the newsstands and in the supermarkets. Of
course, the granddaddy of them all is Think and Grow Rich by Na-

poleon Hill, who interviewed the millionaires of his day in the 1920s. Very little of the book is about making money but rather focuses on the habits and thinking of wealthy people.

Millionaire Mindset

Harv Eckerd is an author and speaker especially noted for one of his books titled, The Millionaire Mindset. His study and research is about how to think like a millionaire by understanding their characteristics and patterns. There is some basic truth to what he has concluded.

Some of the key attributes he shares concern:

- Staying focused

- Finding clarity

- Having the guts for risk

- Finding the knowledge you'll need

- Keeping the right attitude

- Focusing on quality

Having personally worked with many millionaires, we can say that Harv's insights are practical and effective for anyone attempting to achieve their goals, money focused or not.

Harv Eckerd believes he has discovered the patterns that make successful millionaires. He boasts, *"If you follow all these patterns, then the universe will make you rich."* In other words, if you develop these habits of thinking and operating, you will receive riches and just naturally become a millionaire. Wouldn't it be nice if it were that simple?

When Brig has personally spoken to some of these great 'authors of success,' many of who Brig hired to speak at his conferences …they have admitted to him that less than five percent of their readers actually achieve success. Why? Is it fear or hype? Is it because people have dreams but are unwilling to pay the price? The answer is only a few pages away.

"Money is a great servant but a lousy Master."

BRIG HART, CO-FOUNDER OF USA ASSOCIATION

Fame & Notoriety

When you think of famous people, names such as Princess Beatrice, Jim Carrey, Steve Jobs, or Bill Gates may come to mind. Movie stars, entertainers, and athletes always receive the most endorsements and free press, whether they want it or not. Here is an amazing number: There are one billion people that have Facebook accounts. That's more than three times the population of America. People of all ages and walks of life want their moment of fame.

The world perception is that you are successful if you are famous, if you are popular, if you are a cover story, or if you are featured in the media. In fact, John remembers years ago when he went through training at the Chamber of Commerce Institute at the University of Notre Dame, one of the professors lectured about PR and marketing.

He asked us the question, *"What is the most popular page in the largest circulating magazine in America?"* At that time, Parade magazine had the largest circulation in the world. It came out Sunday mornings in your local paper. The page was on the front inside cover, and he thought of it immediately.

It was all about the gossip of movie stars and famous people. People wrote in and asked, *"Is it true that star so and so is remarried?"* Or said, *"Today I heard so and so have moved to Switzerland."* It was a gossip column for the masses with the questions and answers you MUST know.

Most Read Page

It wasn't long after that when emerging entrepreneurs realized the opportunity from Parade's success. People magazine came out, then

Us magazine. Today, we have a number of gossip-filled tabloids vying for our attention at the checkout counter. They beckon us to read about famous people and the good and not-so-good events of their lives. Soon to follow were TV shows like Entertainment Tonight, Inside Edition, and Extra. All attempted to grab our attention several times a week. Those featured on the programs became the role models for far too many in the world.

This inner passion to emulate those we admire is a driving passion. Young people ask, *"Who's going to be the next American Idol?"* While adults yearn to be rich, famous, and powerful. The media knows this, and they exaggerate it on the screen to keep us watching. They cater to the burning desire in all us to achieve a level of success or notoriety and be recognized as 'someone special.'

Jay Leno, the late night TV comedian, during a serious moment, once said, *"If it bleeds, it leads."* He explains that too many people are misled and sucked into sensationalism and led down the wrong path in life.

The hunger is for attention. *"Babies cry for it, and men die for it."* What feeds this insatiable desire? Insecurity. In fact, psychologists might say the pursuit of being famous is a reaching out to be accepted or acknowledged. Yet, it turns out to be more of a curse than a blessing?

Possessions

So, how big, important, or exclusive is your sports car? Your boat? Your second or third home on the beach or in the mountains? Your club seats for your NFL team? Or your weekend shuttle to the French Riviera? And how well are you surpassing the Joneses?

We've all seen the bumper sticker: 'He who dies with the most toys wins.' Obviously, there's not a lot of validity to that, but it is the vivid image created in our minds by the media. Buy into that perspective, and you may continue to chase success that eludes you. It is characterized in the old TV program, *"Lifestyles of the Rich and Famous,"* which displays the lavish homes and toys acquired by the ridiculously wealthy.

You have probably heard of Elvis Presley, Hugh Hefner, and Aristotle Onassis—three men with lavish estates, possessions, and yachts. They seemed to enjoy and use them in order to magnify their image. In fact, some of their possessions were servants and an entourage of people needed to complete them. Both of us have been in homes of wealthy individuals who had twenty cars. Some they drove. Others were classic models that they simply showed off. Often rich car collectors even have mechanics that live in the guesthouse with some of the servants.

For thirteen years, Johnwas fortunate to own the license to TEC in Florida, The Executive Committee (now known as Vistage), where he helped CEOs learn to be more effective in leading their business. For his annual meeting in 1988, he selected Sam Walton, the founder of Wal-Mart, as his choice for 'Entrepreneur of the Year.' After contacting him and inviting him to receive the award, Sam wrote John a personal letter thanking him and explaining that he couldn't come to Florida to accept the award. The reason? He had a more important date to go hunting with his dog.

Sam had the reputation of driving the same pickup truck he'd had for many years. Some would find this amazing from the man who founded one of the biggest corporations in the world. Amazingly, even though his business had enormous buying power, he preferred to keep a very modest lifestyle. While many corporate executives justify their own jets, Sam personally flew his Piper Cub aircraft to visit stores and scout for new store locations. That's the reason Sam never made it on the 'Lifestyles of the Rich and Famous' even though he became one of the richest men in America.

Power

The passion for power is the ultimate ego trip. For many, being in control is the fastest way to the top. We strive to be successful on our own terms.

Frank Sinatra, one of the most popular singers of the 20th century, sang, *"My Way."* Notice the lyrics.

And now the end is near,
and so I face the final curtain.

My friend I'll say it clear,
I'll state my case of which I am certain.

I've lived a life that is full.
I've tracked every highway, and more, much more than this,

I did it my way.

I have loved, I have laughed and cried,
had my fill and my share of losing.

And now as tears subside,
I find it all so amusing.

To think I did all that, not in a shy way.
I did it my way.

For what is a man, what does he have,
if not himself, then he has not.

To say the things he truly feels,
and not the words of one who kneels.

Let the record show, I took the blows
and did it my way.

In other words, if you want success and power, do it your way. This accurately characterizes an attitude and way of thinking in the world's model for power, fame and wealth.

One of today's poster children of success from the world's perspective is Donald Trump. Brig met him and had him speak for him. Personally, we don't know his heart. But from a media perspective, making money appears to be his mission and measure for life. Money, power, fame, and possessions—Donald has all four. He is the super model for worldly success ? And if you don't line up with what he wants, You're Fired! That's what the world's model of success and power is—being in control.

"If pride is the greatest sin, then humility is the greatest virtue"

BRIG HART, CO-FOUNDER OF THE USA ASSOCIATION

CHAPTER 2

The Founders' Perspective of the American Dream

There is an alternative perspective and model for achieving the American dream. In fact, it is significantly different than the worldly model, but offers true riches, not just financial but the peace and satisfaction impacting others for a divine purpose.

Here are some key words and phases from the Declaration of Independence...

When in the Course of human events, it becomes necessary for one people to dissolve the political bands...

To assume among the powers of the earth, the separate and equal station to which the Laws of Nature and of Nature's God entitle them...

We hold these truths to be self-evident, that all men are created equal, that they are endowed by their Creator with certain unalienable Rights, that among these are Life, Liberty and the pursuit of Happiness.

This perspective asserts that individual rights are based in the belief that there is a purpose and calling in each of our lives for *'Life, Liberty and pursuit of Happiness.'* It was our founding fathers that set in motion the ground rules and principles that would create freedom and values. Their set of beliefs actually changed the course of history. They believed that they had a divine purpose and used the Bible as their guide to declare freedom. They believed that Freedom was granted to all people from God beginning with Adam and Eve. This ultimately led to creating a constitution that has become a model for other nations.

Our Free Enterprise System is based on the freedom and principles of our founding fathers for the fullness and pursuit of happiness. It gives people the opportunity for happiness by self-initiative, faith and risk.

Stephen Covey, in his highly accepted book, *The 7 Habits of Highly Effective People* popularized the statement *"always keep the end in mind."* His point is that you should set your goal, then work your way backwards, laying out the action steps you need to take to get there. This isn't new, but it is valid. All good meeting planners, corporate leaders, and strategic planners have used this concept for years.

Vision for Freedom

Success it not necessarily about acquiring wealth but maximizing our lives for the greatest good. Ben Franklin and Thomas Jefferson, who guided the writing of our Constitution, saw this as the key. It's not about religion or denominations, but sound doctrines that impact people and change lives for the better. Franklin didn't fully recognize that freedom along with the values and principles of the Bible would create the world's best economic model.

Even if you are not a Bible believer, there is great power and truth in this idea. If you don't want to believe this perspective, just hold on because as you delve into the timeless truths throughout the book, you will recognize gems of wisdom that empower you to be tremendously successful in any endeavor.

In comparing the world's model with our founders' perspective, consider the following questions:

- Are you called to be rich or resourceful?

- Are you called to be a superstar or a servant?

- Are you called to be famous or faithful?

- Are you called to be successful or significant?

As Bob Buford, a very wealthy businessman and author of **Half Time** said. *"When you really think about it, is the world's model hype or truth? Is it to sell newspapers or to help you achieve all you are called to be?"*

Nearly 90 percent of Americans believe there is a God who is full of love for us and that we all have a distinct place in making the world better. Even those that sell the world's perspective often recognize the hidden truth in their hype: That helping people accomplish things is far more important than making money, finding fame, or obtaining power. Our founders went through trying times, did their research, and prayed for the right way to create a nation.

The Bible says:

> *"For the wisdom of this world is foolishness in God's sight."*

> *"What good will it be for a man if he gains the whole world yet he forfeits his soul?"*

> *"As it is, you do not belong to the world, but I have chosen you out of the world."*

The words of the Bible are saying we are to live *"IN this world but not be OF the world."* We are to be an integral part of the Lord's calling and grand design. This life on earth is very short compared to life in eternity. So, our perspective needs to be adjusted to the long term. The Bible calls us to make a choice. Either follow our own path or the path He designed for us, which is based on His ways and principles.

The founding fathers' perspective is rooted in relationships. The world's view is all about performance and our own self-determined desire. That is not to say that if we follow the world's view, we can't achieve success and be used for divine purpose. The difference involves perspective and relationships, because the founding fathers' model is based on relationships, mission, and obedience.

The traits our founding fathers valued were:

- Knowing our purpose and mission

- Developing loving relationships

- Being obedient to the grand design

What the founding father's said...

About the Christian principles they used to create our Constitution and Culture of the USA

Thomas Jefferson, SIGNER OF THE DECLARATION OF INDEPENDENCE; DIPLOMAT; GOVERNOR OF VIRGINIA; SECRETARY OF STATE; THIRD PRESIDENT OF THE UNITED STATES	*"The doctrines of Jesus are simple, and tend all to the happiness of man."* *"I am a Christian in the only sense in which He wished anyone to be: sincerely attached to His doctrines in preference to all others."* *"I am a real Christian—that is to say, a disciple of the doctrines of Jesus Christ."*

Patrick Henry, REVOLUTIONARY GENERAL; LEGISLATOR; "THE VOICE OF LIBERTY"; RATIFIER OF THE U. S. CONSTITUTION; GOVERNOR OF VIRGINIA	*"Being a Christian... is a character which I prize far above all this world has or can boast."* *"The Bible... is a book worth more than all the other books that were ever printed."* *"Righteousness alone can exalt America as a nation. Whoever thou art, remember this; and in thy sphere practice virtue thyself, and encourage it in others."* *"The great pillars of all government and of social life [are] virtue, morality, and religion. This is the armor, my friend, and this alone, that renders us invincible."*
Daniel Webster, U. S. SENATOR; SECRETARY OF STATE; "DEFENDER OF THE CONSTITUTION"	*"[T]he Christian religion—its general principles—must ever be regarded among us as the foundation of civil society. Whatever makes men good Christians, makes them good citizens. The Bible is a book... which teaches man his own individual responsibility, his own dignity, and his equality with his fellow man."*

| **George Washington,** JUDGE; MEMBER OF THE CONTINENTAL CONGRESS; COMMANDER-IN-CHIEF OF THE CONTINENTAL ARMY; PRESIDENT OF THE CONSTITUTIONAL CONVENTION; FIRST PRESIDENT OF THE UNITED STATES; "FATHER OF HIS COUNTRY" | *"You do well to wish to learn our arts and ways of life, and above all, the religion of Jesus Christ. These will make you a greater and happier people than you are."*

"I now make it my earnest prayer that God would... most graciously be pleased to dispose us all to do justice, to love mercy, and to demean ourselves with that charity, humility, and pacific temper of the mind which were the characteristics of the Divine Author of our blessed religion." |
| **Benjamin Franklin,** SIGNER OF THE DECLARATION; DIPLOMAT; PRINTER; SCIENTIST; SIGNER OF THE CONSTITUTION; GOVERNOR OF PENNSYLVANIA | *"As to Jesus of Nazareth, my opinion of whom you particularly desire, I think the system of morals and His religion as He left them to us, the best the world ever saw or is likely to see."* |

SOURCE: WALLBUILDERS WACO, TEXAS

Captial Recognition

According to the Providence Foundation, *"America's monuments and symbols contain the declaration that the source of our birth, liberty, and greatness is God."*

Here are some examples:

The Library of Congress—A Gutenberg Bible and the other a hand-copied Giant Bible of Mainz where President Andrew Jackson said, "The Bible is the rock upon which our republic rests."

Many Biblical inscriptions can be found on the ceiling and walls including: *"The light shineth in darkness, and the darkness comprehendeth it not"*; and *"Wisdom is the principal thing therefore get wisdom and with all thy getting, get understanding."*

In the Main Reading Room are statues and quotes representing fields of knowledge.

Moses and Paul represent Religion, with the inscription, *"What doth the Lord require of thee, but to do justly, and to love mercy and to walk humbly with thy God."*

Science is represented by, *"The heavens declare the glory of God; and the firmament showeth His handiwork."*

History: *"One God, one law, one element, and one far-off divine event, to which the whole creation moves."*

The Supreme Court— The Biblical foundation of American law is evidenced throughout this building. On the outside East Pediment is a marble relief of Moses holding tablets containing the Ten Commandments. Engraved on the oak doors at the entrance of the Court Chamber are the Roman numerals I through X, and above the heads of the Justices is a carved marble relief with a large stone tablet containing I through X in between two allegorical figures, representing The Power of Government and The Majesty of the Law (each set of numerals represents ancient law, that is the 10 commandments). In the main foyer are marble busts of previous Chief Justices, many of whom were Christians such as John Jay, the first Chief Justice, and John Marshall, the most prominent in the early years.

Each day the Court is in session, a crier ends his call announcing the formal opening by declaring, *"God save the United States and the Honorable Court."*

The Capitol Building—All of the eight large paintings in the Rotunda present aspects of our Christian history. A few include:

The Landing of Columbus—Columbus said he was convinced to sail because *"it was the Lord who put into my mind"* and that *"the Gospel must still be preached to so many lands."*

The Baptism of Pocahontas—This shows the baptism of one of the first converts in the Virginia colony. The Virginia charter said they came to propagate the *"Christian Religion to such People, as yet live in Darkness of the true knowledge and worship of God."*

Departure of the Pilgrims from Holland—shows the Pilgrims observing a day of prayer and fasting. William Brewster is holding an open Bible upon which is written: *"The New Testament of our Lord and Savior Jesus Christ"* and *"God With Us"* is written on the ship's sail.

Also in the Rotunda are carved reliefs including:

Penn's Treaty with the Indians—Penn called his colony *"a holy experiment"* and said of it that *"my God that has given it to me . . . will, I believe, bless and make it the seed of a nation."*

The Landing of the Pilgrims—*"having undertaken for the Glory of God and advancement of the Christian faith."*

"In God We Trust," our national motto, is inscribed in letters of gold behind the Speaker's rostrum in the House Chamber. Also in this chamber, above the central Gallery door, is a marble relief of Mo-

ses, the greatest of 23 noted law-givers (and the only one full-faced). In 1867 the House Chamber was the meeting place for the largest Church congregation in America. This was not unusual for Churches had been meeting in the Capitol from its beginning.

Statues of many early leaders are displayed throughout the Capitol. Most of these people were Christians (and many were ministers), including George Washington, James Garfield, Samuel Adams, Rev. Peter Muhlenberg, Rev. Roger Williams, and many more.

Many plaques in the Capitol declare our faith as well, including: In God We Trust, placed above the Senate main door; *"What hath God Wrought!"* — the first message sent over the telegraph in 1844, found on the Samuel F.B. Morse Plaque outside old Supreme Court Chamber.

The Prayer Room contains an open Bible sitting on an altar in front of a stained window showing Washington in earnest prayer. Behind him is etched the first verse of Psalm 16, *"Preserve me, O God, for in Thee do I put my trust."*

The National Archives—A bronze design on the floor of the Rotunda contains the Ten Commandments with Senate and Justice to the right of them, which symbolizes that our legal system has its origin in God's law. The two most important civil documents on display reflect Biblical principles of government.

These are:

The Declaration of Independence (1776)—contains such ideas as man is created in the Divine image, all men are equal, man is superior to the state, the state exists for man.

The United States Constitution (1787)—Christian ideas include: the reign of law; trial by jury of peers under law; Creator endowed rights, not government granted; Christian self-government; religious freedom; private property rights.

The Washington Monument—From the tallest structure in Washington a message of Praise be to God goes forth. Engraved upon the aluminum capstone on the top of this 555 foot monument is Laus Deo. Inside the structure are carved tribute blocks with many Godly messages: *"Holiness to the Lord," "Search the Scriptures," "The memory of the just is blessed," "May Heaven to this union continue its beneficence," "In God We Trust," "Train up a child in the way he should go, and when he is old, he will not depart from it."*

The White House—An inscription by the first President to inhabit the White House, John Adams, is cut into the marble facing of the State Dining Room fireplace. It reads: *"I pray Heaven to Bestow the Best of Blessings on THIS HOUSE and on All that shall hereafter Inhabit it. May none but Honest and Wise Men ever rule under this Roof."* Each President has attended church, associated with the Christian faith, taken the oath of office with their hand on a Bible, and referred to God in their inaugural addresses.

The Lincoln Memorial—The words engraved upon the walls of the Lincoln Memorial reflect the Christian faith and providential perspective of our 16th President, Abraham Lincoln. On the south wall is the Gettysburg Address which ends exclaiming *"that this nation, under God, shall have a new birth of freedom—and that government of the people, by the people, and for the people, shall not perish from the earth."* On the wall of the north chamber is Lincoln's Second Inaugural Address which shows his knowledge of the Scriptures: (Matthew 18:7).

The Jefferson Memorial—The author of the Declaration of Independence and America's third President, Thomas Jefferson, though unorthodox is some of his religious views, claimed to be a Christian, attended church throughout his life, and held to a Biblical world view, which is reflected in the inscriptions in the memorial. The excerpt from the Declaration speaks of Creator endowed rights. The inscription from Jefferson's Virginia Statute for Religious Freedom states: *"Almighty God hath created the mind free. All attempts to*

*influence it by temporal punishments or burthens . . . are a depar-
ture from the plan of the Holy Author of our religion. . . . All men
shall be free to profess and by argument to maintain, their opinions in matters of religion."* A third inscription from his Notes of the
State of Virginia says: *"God who gave us life gave us liberty. Can
the liberties of a nation be secure when we have removed a conviction that these liberties are the gift of God? Indeed I tremble for my
country when I reflect that God is just, that his justice cannot sleep
forever."*

There are many other monuments and buildings in Washington that
proclaim America's faith in God.

At Arlington National Cemetery, the Tomb of the Unknown Soldier
monument, carved from a single rectangular block of marble to
honor unknown soldiers who gave their life for the cause of liberty, bears the inscription: HERE RESTS IN HONORED GLORY
AN AMERICAN SOLDIER KNOWN BUT TO GOD.

On the front facade of Union Station three Scripture verses are engraved: *"Thou has put all things under his feet." "The truth shall
make you free." "The desert shall rejoice and blossom like the
rose."*

Conclusion

In the words of the U.S. House of Representatives in 1854: "The
great vital element in our system is the belief of our people in the
pure doctrines and divine truths of the gospel of Jesus Christ." We
as a nation must not forget that God is the author of our liberty, for
if we do we shall lose it."

Knowing Our Purpose

The older we get, the more we realize that success is based upon
using our God-given talents and following His plan, not our own. It
took John four years of playing high school football to discover that

he was not as good as he thought. Even though he dreamed of playing in college, the college scouts never offered him a scholarship and
verified he wouldn't make the cut.

"You can be anything you want to be!" So say many athletes and
well-intended authors. Unfortunately, that is not true! To his dis-
may, he discovered that his body, lack of speed, and many other
attributes proved that the college scouts were right, no matter how
much it broke his heart.

The grand design for John has always been to be in business. While
he has been diverted at times by his own dreams, he has learned to
see how those experiences served a greater plan he may not have
been unable to recognize at the time. Garth Brooks was right in his
song, *"Thank God for Unanswered Prayers."* It's a song about him
going to his high school reunion and seeing a former crush. He recalls praying deeply for God to bring them together. Seeing her at
the reunion, he thanks God that He led him down a different and
better path.

We can all recall things that we desperately wanted to happen. In the
end, they would not have been good for us. Our Designer wants to
unfold His plan for us, but we must be open and mature to receive it.
We must be willing to accept and learn about our purpose.

At this point, you may be unwilling to accept the founding fathers'
perspective. But God does not write you off or forget you. Instead,
He reveals these divine truths through authors of the how-to-get-
rich books. In fact, they offer hope and expand our thinking. Our
Creator has a purpose for these writers and even uses their worldly
success message to move us forward in life, even if we are not ready
to know His plan. Yet, at some point—through tough or touching
circumstances—we eventually become open to God. He convicts our
hearts to get us on track with His plan. Amazingly, He waits for us to
be open without condemnation.

The fact of the matter is that when we die, we cannot take our money and wealth with us. All the monetary 'stuff' has no value in heaven or hell. It may make big news from a worldly perspective, but in the final analysis, it is temporary compared to the eternal and relational aspects of life.

Loving Relationships

The second part of our founding fathers' model is about loving relationships. When Jesus was asked, *"What is the greatest commandment?"*, He said that the first is to love God and the second is to love one another. Bottom line: This is man's greatest failure.

It began with Adam and Eve not honoring God. In other words, disobedience is equal to not loving Him. But through God's grace and mercy, He revised His plan to grant man free will. So, we are born with the freedom to follow our own path and to live independently of His purpose. This is one of the reasons that our founding fathers wanted to create a nation of freedom, something no king or dictator had ever done.

> They acknowledged their belief in God and that He chose to work through man in a free society. Yet, they recognized that freedom had to have standards for men to respect one another.

The first four of the Ten Commandments lay down the ground rules for a personal and spiritual relationship with Him. (The Ten Commandments are chiseled above the benches of the Supreme Court Justices in Washington, D.C.) The individual relationships of the founding fathers with the Lord are documented and profound. Wall Builders, a research group out of Waco, Texas has studied the proceeding of the Continental Congress members. They have proof of prayers that lasted as long as two hours at the beginnings of meetings with guest pastors and chaplains.

Ten Commandments

Spiritual Laws *are about having a relationship*

between God and us personally

1. *Have no other god's before*—Don't place you before Me in pride but be humble, seek and trust Me.

2. *Have no false idols*—Don't worship or become addicted to activities, substances, things or deceit. Become convicted and ask for forgiveness of trying to replace Me. I am still here with you.

3. *Do not use God's name in vain*—But praise by your words.

4. *Keep the Sabbath Holy*—Rest, listen and learn IN relationship with Me.

Ben Franklin is quoted as reminding the members of the Constitutional Convention, through times of bickering and delays that *"Our prayers, were heard and they were graciously answered in winning the War of Independence."* Franklin passionately urged them to pray daily for spiritual guidance from above, both personally and at the beginning of each session led by a clergyman. They researched together, found their principles, and laid the foundation for a new nation in the Bible.

The next six of the Ten Commandments are about having a loving relationship with our neighbor. All of this is about a moral code of respectfully interacting with one another and how we treat our fellow man, regardless of our differences. It is often characterized as the Golden Rule, *"Do unto others as you would have them do unto you."*

Ten Commandments continued:

Moral Laws *Jesus said,*

"Love your neighbor"

5. *Honor your father and mother*—Respect the authority of others, just as you would in your own family.

6. *Do not murder*—Forgive and value the lives of others.

7. *Do not commit adultery*—Be faithful and loyal to those in relationship to you.

8. *Do no steal*—But give to others.

9. *Do not bear false witness*—Earn respect through your honesty and integrity.

10. *Do not covet*—Appreciate the differences and diversity in one another. Be an encourager.

You can see the founding fathers, past Presidents and congresses built upon these foundations through the Bill of Rights and our Constitution. First they dealt with Freedom. Spirituality was a personal issue and with Religious freedom there would be no limiting people in how they worshiped God by dominations or other faiths (which other nations have done). More aggressively they chose to protect the Moral rights of people—protecting them from citizen's violating the rights of others. i.e. stealing, lying, prejudice, murder and authority issues through our Bill of Rights, laws and justice system. Even our court system originated from the Book of Judges in the Bible.

Biblical Guide

Who are our neighbors anyway? As a kid, we both remember asking our mom and dad one day after going to church, *"Who are our neighbors? How can we love them?"* We continued by asking, *"We don't even know them, do we?"*

Our neighbors are the people we interact with in business, home, community or school. If you're running a business, they are your customers, suppliers, vendors, employees, stockholders, and community leaders. In a larger context, everybody is our neighbor. From the perspective of our founding fathers, this concept is critical to our success. It is also an essential element that is skipped over by *"preachers"* of the world's view. Yet, John once read an article in the magazine of Bank of America, which talked about the Golden Rule for treating customers and suppliers. With good intent, it can be a significant issue the bigger a company gets—an issue we will touch on later through examples.

The Bible urges us to leave this world with no grudges, resentments, or even enemies. Leave here with nothing but friends.

John has often quoted an example from Laura Nash's book, *Believers in Business,* of the young man who was very frustrated with his boss. He did not respect him and knew he had addiction problems. He told his Bible study group he was going to quit his job because of his boss. They suggested praying for his boss first. That irritated him, but he decided to do it anyway. And—the more he prayed, the more his heart changed toward the man. He then started to build a good relationship with him. And—in time, his boss was terminated and the company asked the young man to take his place. Bottom line: Prayer and love works much better than hate and resentment.

"Faith and Risk
are opposite sides of the same coin"

Love is the Key

In Gary Chapman's book, *The 5 Love Languages,* he describes how each of us has a different understanding of love. The five love languages are represented by

1. Words of affirmation

2. Quality time, listening

3. Acts of service

4. Gifts

5. Physical touch

In business growth, we can also show love through:

• Providing good services (an enjoyable experience where they want to return or tell others),

• Quality products (they can trust and can rely on again)

• Listening to our customers, vendors, suppliers, employees, and community.

If you do these things with good character and integrity, you create a powerful economic exchange—and produce profits. In fact, making money over time is the result of building relationships with all our customers and friends.

Peter Drucker, the most famous business guru of the last century, simply stated the purpose of a business is *"finding the need of a customer and filling it."* In essence, he reaffirms the Golden Rule for a business and stressing the importance of building relationships.

Howard Schultz sees the romance in coffee and its power in bringing people together. Howard built the Starbucks Coffee Company chain of stores around the world. According to Howard, *"If you take care of the soft side of your business, namely your people, and you treat the customer with a passion for what you offer them, you will be profitable. The customer will see you are sincere and return over and over again."* Can you see and hear his love and passion to serve the customer through good relationships?

Jim Penney, founder of J.C. Penney department store chain said, *"The number one management training course is found in the Bible. It's called the Sermon on the Mount." He also said "making money must always be a by-product of building the character of men and women and rendering of essential service to mankind."*

It is really about how we're to love our neighbor. It is about our attitude, heart, and humility. It is about how we are to interact with other people to influence them for good through the sale of quality merchandise and service. That is what brings customers back repeatedly. The same principles apply in a marriage, family, school, or church. Loving relationships are rooted in how people interact and show love toward one another.

Being Obedient to the Grand Design

The founding fathers came to realize that initiating and winning the war for independence was through the call, conviction, and grace of God. Through great struggle and sacrifice, they knew they must be obedient to the Lord's plan to create a new nation founded on freedom and His principles. All 56 signers of the Declaration of Independence put their lives, families, farms, and properties in jeopardy. What they signed was an act of treason. Nine lost their lives during the war, and nearly two thirds lost everything they had.

Nearly every act of righteous obedience is from the call and conviction of God upon our heart. Abraham Lincoln knew he was called and convicted to be obedient through public service. He had 12 consecutive defeats over 29 years before finally being elected President of the United States. Many of us would have given up and lost faith. Where would our nation be without Lincoln's selfless act of obedience and sacrifice? It was through the same conviction of God and act of obedience that led Martin Luther King, Jr. to lead a non-violent revolution for equality. Amazingly, years later, it was the same spirit that lead one of his adversaries, former Governor George Wallace, to seek public forgiveness for the wrongful stance he took in attempting to prevent the civil rights movement.

In 1952, Conrad Hilton, founder of the Hilton Hotel Chain, felt so convicted to make our nation aware of the threat of Communism that he risked his personal credibility and the success of his hotel business. He believed the threat was so great that he placed full-page ads in the Saturday Evening Post and many other major magazines and newspapers. The ads pictured Uncle Sam on his knees asking God for forgiveness and to save us from ourselves. After our victories in the world wars and the following economic stability, he felt we were soft and arrogant toward the great threat of communism. Was his act of obedience rewarded through the growth of his enterprise or in other ways? The Bible says that the prayers of a righteous man will avail much. This is part of the heritage he left his hotel chain and those who still work there today.

Well Done, Faithful Servant

The mission of every Christian is to get to heaven and hear these words, *"Well done, good and faithful servant."* Our journey is designed to discover the plan He has for us. Yes, some find it quickly because their gifts and talents draw them to it. Others back into it without fully receiving a confirmation because they have no intention of seeking God and spiritual wisdom.

Many seek Him through personal commitment and hear His voice. Millard Fuller was a millionaire at 29 and had all the possessions, fame, and money he ever needed, but he did not have love. His wife had left him because she never saw him. Heartbroken, he turned to the Lord and told his wife he would give it all up and seek the Lord to serve His purpose. Together, they sought the Lord and found God's calling in Americus, Georgia. Every day for 30 years, they prayed for guidance as they founded and built Habitat for Humanity. Today, with the cooperation of thousands of people, they have built more than 300,000 houses for over a million needy people around the world.

Jesus followed God with all His heart. In obedience, He did whatever the Father told him. After 33 years of human life, he was tortured and hung on a cross to die for all of our sins. Yet His life did not revolve around power, prestige, and possessions. He was homeless by today's standards, yet the center of His ministry was the relationships He developed with family, friends, enemies and those He touched. Teaching, preaching, and praying were simple in comparison. Jesus said, *"Greater love has no man than this, that he lay down his life for his friends."*

Acts of Obedience

Through acts of obedience, we leave our legacy by sacrificing our time, talent, and treasures. In 1980, Candy Lightner lost her daughter to a drunk driver. Out of a burning heart and act of obedience, she vowed that her daughter's death would not be in vain. She dedicated her life getting laws passed through her organization, Mothers Against Drunk Driving (MADD). Through her efforts, this organization has had an enormous impact on national, state, and local laws and the lives of millions of drivers and their families.

When it comes to achieving success in life or business, who is smarter? —You or the One who created you? The song, *"My Way,"* emphasizes self-centered attitudes and mocks God when it says, *"For what is a man, what has he got? If not himself, then he has not. To say the things he truly feels, and not the words of the one who kneels."*

In contrast, you can picture Jesus kneeling in prayer to the Father and saying *"Our Father, who art in Heaven."*

When all is said and done, real success is found through obedience to the will and calling of the One who created us.

Life is battle between good and evil.
God and satan work through people.

Being blessed is an attitude

According to Author Os Hillman, *"both God and satan want you dead."* Satan wants you dead and gone so God can't use you and God wants you dead to yourself and dependent on Him.

God is using mankind to build goodness which allows man to be obedient and to be fulfilled in his love, family, work and opportunities to help change the world. He forgave our sins through Jesus Christ who died for our sins and to break the power of evil for all who accept Him as Savior and Lord. Satan works on our thinking trying to lead us to frustration, fear, depression, sickness, suicide or death. Murderers who go on rampages to kill innocent people with guns, baseball bats or other weapons are led by the hateful thoughts that satan fills there mind with notice how most of them kill themselves also.

Every believer who works to share their faith will face battles that many unbelievers will never see. But 'attitude' will overcome most obstacles whether you believe or not. If you aren't up for the battle and trials that will come and get worse, you will have it much worse. Ask yourself, are my trials and obstacles worse than Christ faced.

He was spit upon, cursed, beaten and killed on a cross for you and me to have a better life and opportunity. My toughest defeats could never match that experience.

Take heart because the Bible says, *"the battle is not ours, but the Lords."* We must trust in Him and be willing to fight and not quit and be patient in our calling. The fulfillment of God's visions never transpires as fast as we would like.

We are to use our gifts and talents to be obedient. The Lord hates the slothful (laziness), as He said when the farmer rejected the person who buried his gift rather than investing it. When the others produced a big return, the master cursed the one who buried his gift (Matthew 25:26)

> 16 *You did not choose me, but I chose you and*
> *appointed you so that you might go and bear fruit—*
> *fruit that will last—and so that whatever you ask in my name*
> *the Father will give you.*
> — John 15:16 (NIV)

CHAPTER 3

Confirming the Foundational Truth

Whom Do You Trust? So here is the big question: Which view can we trust? The world's view or the founding fathers' perspective? We contend that the decision of our founding fathers is the best choice. Ultimately, the world's view and the American dream is only successful because of the Lord's principles of free will, grace, character, and morality. Without them, there would be little financial success, possessions, power, and fame. Freedom and grace allow these things. The world's perspective is mixed with hype, false impressions, ignorance, and media deceit based on a self-centered focus rather than one based on love.

Yes, good performance in business and life is also derived from working hard. Meeting goals is part of God's plan. The real issue involves which force is driving us: The passion for self-focused success or the passion to serve God and others. What really impels us toward success? What are our true motives?

My point is that all personal and business success is under girded by the truths, plans, and grace of God. Indeed, even these truths apply to the atheist. God loves the non-believer as much as He loves you or me. Nothing in this world is successful without His grace. God's grace is unmerited favor upon us even when we don't deserve it.

Harv Eckerd and so many authors of 'hype' are either sincerely ignorant or share their limited view in order to sell popular books. Their claim of an 'attraction factor' is based on aspects of biblical truth but creates the false notion that the universe will make you rich. This ultimately misleads people from the truth of God's Word. While the 'get rich' authors inspire and encourage risk taking, they seldom share the whole truth. They are not based on truth but a distortion of truth, what many would call deceit.

> *"Success is not measured by what you are compared to others: Success is measured by what you are compared to what you could be."*
>
> — BILL GOTHARD

A Testimony for Freedom

From a Biblical perspective there are 5 Basic types of Freedom... Religious, Political, Economic, Freedom of Expression and Freedom in Christ. God is drawing us away from bondage and fear and toward Freedom (both physical and mental) so we can maximize our gifts and talents and achieve our ultimate potential.

As the Lord brings the world together, nations will no longer be able to be islands. We are already interconnected economically, and as Economic Freedom strengthens in these countries we will do more business together.

In 2011, a New York Times writer wrote about the death of Steve Jobs. It was also the beginning of Syrian unrest and passion of the young to demonstrate and fight for freedom for from their dictator. He quoted a young Syrian girl's opinion. She knew Steve's biological father was Syrian. She said, *"If Steve Jobs had been born with freedom here in our country, Apple would have been invented in Syria and helped to change the world."*

Immigrants still come to the USA because they know there is more opportunity here than any other nation. What God ultimately wants is for His people to become all they are called to be. Dictators, Communist and even Muslim-type cultures limit people from using their gifts, talents and leadership abilities to create new organizations to help make a better world.

Deceit is a Problem

Deceit takes truth and blends it with what is false. For example, we all agree that if you work hard with determination, you can achieve a level of success, but no one gets there alone. It reinforces that faulty notion that you can be anything you want to be.

Yes, God gives us talents and eventually an inner desire to use them. But anything is a deceitful and misleading word. The anything philosophy does not work if we are not designed for that purpose. We can have a self- directed passion to be a successful entrepreneur, but it won't happen in 'any' business, anymore than wanting to fly and jumping off a cliff will work.

The Bible is rooted in the principles that God gave to Moses and the insight He gave to King Solomon (the richest man in the world) as well as to the prophets, the disciples, and so many others. But Jesus made the difference. He brought grace and a much deeper understanding of God's laws through the "Spirit of the Law" along with profound and simpler interpretations of truth, success, and even failure.

By now, it should be simple for you to determine that we believe we must trust our founding fathers. They are the ones who sacrificed and knew their calling to create the greatest and most prosperous nation on earth. While there is some value in the worldly perspective, it is only half-truth, a fleeting truth, and is not based on eternal truth. Through worldly determination, we can achieve much, but every 'grace period' runs out in time.

Finding the Source for True Success

We need a standard to live by to determine true success. The Bible says that God is a Spirit of truth. Truth is a set of standards filled with direction and purpose. Frank Peretti, the author of This Present Darkness says, *"Truth is truth whether you believe it or not. Truth is truth whether you have heard it or not. And, truth is truth whether you like it or not."* There are sets of ultimate truths in the Bible that are guidelines for changing hearts, families, businesses, cultures, and even nations.

Roger Babson, the 1920's author of Fundamentals of Prosperity, interviewed the President of Argentina and asked why South America, with all its natural resources, was so far behind North America in terms of progress and marketing. The President replied, *"I came to the conclusion, South America was settled by the Spanish who came in search of gold, but North America was settled by Pilgrim Fathers who went in search of God."*

Whether we are believers in the Bible or are non-believers, we have a common problem. We are trapped in our existing journey, belief, and knowledge base. The Bible says, *"My people perish for lack of knowledge."*

Jesus' biggest adversaries were the Pharisees. They were trapped in their own thinking, interprtations, judgments and sins—not knowing the depth of the truth of the Lord.

We acquire our insights and knowledge from friends, teachers, role models, and trials in our journey through life. Good or bad, we are all on a quest like the pilgrims and founding fathers to find the truth for our life and those we influence. The question is: Are we truly seeking the real truth that sets us free to be successful in life.

Without a doubt, the Bible is our best standard. The Lord speaks through His Word. That is why it is called *"The Living Bible."* It's called living because the Holy Spirit (our comforter, teacher and revealer) talks to the true believer with new insights and direction. But if we are not spiritually connected and tuned to the right frequency, it makes no more sense than the worldly logic or limited reason we already have.

1 Corinthians 2:14 *"The person without the Spirit does not accept the things that come from the Spirit of God but considers them foolishness, and cannot understand them because they are discerned only through the Spirit. 15 The person with the Spirit makes judgments about all things, but such a person is not subject to merely human judgments."*

Three Cornerstones

In writing his first book, True Wealth by the Book, John was seeking to understand what the Bible was saying about business success. He discovered through praying for wisdom and studying the Word that God has a design for building a business on a solid foundation of three cornerstones:

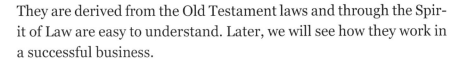

1. Character,

2. Moral, and

3. Spiritual Truth.

They are derived from the Old Testament laws and through the Spirit of Law are easy to understand. Later, we will see how they work in a successful business.

Our point is that we would have never discovered these and the principles of this book without the Spirit of God working through biblical teachings. When the Holy Spirit is speaking to you it is like listening to an interpreter—showing you the application and wisdom you need to change or help others.

Once you begin to understand the practical business language of the

Bible, it starts to flow without having to think. Moved along by the Spirit, you share insights as it flows through you. For instance, John and wife spent some time in Brazil many years ago. When I finally could think in Portuguese, it flowed easily versus trying to interpret from English first.

He often sees businesses dying from leaders that do not know what they are doing. Sadly, they are not seeking the Bible for answers. They do not seek the wise counsel of others. They do not pray for guidance. Instead, most hold onto their worldly thinking and never seek the depth of what God is trying to say to them. Without openness, there is no soil for growth in their lives or businesses.

According to a pastor friend of mine, some people have committed suicide after receiving test results, showing that they are dying from cancer. They took their own lives before getting a second opinion or looking for another alternative to improve their health. In one case, the lab discovered that they made a mistake, but the information came too late. Research indicates that nearly 35 percent of sickness, surgery, and prescriptions are misdiagnosed. In other words, human beings make mistakes and wrongly read test results a predictable amount of time.

The Guide for Billions

Look around! God is moving in the world and is involved in all of our lives whether we believe it or not. His principles are found in the Bible. It influences billions of people around the world every day. It is the greatest book ever written. It is a living document of God's love, power, and wisdom. People gain wisdom and insight as they seek the Author to understand His ways. The Word of God is like a seed planted in the soil of our hearts, growing like a flowering branch that brings inner peace, comfort, direction, and depth to our lives.

Family members give Bibles to their teens, friends, and relatives. Churches and missionaries buy Bibles for people all around the world. Why do we have such an appetite for the Bible? The answer is because it speaks to our hearts and gives us direction. It inspires us, gives us comfort, and provides hope for living. It also changes our aspirations and us.

> **The Bible is translated into**
> **more than 2,000 languages.**
> **The next most translated text is Shakespeare,**
> **with only 50 languages.**

Every year, there are another 20-30 new language translations for different tribes and dialects. There are ministries like Wycliffe that have the heart and calling to do such translations. There are people who specifically go into Indian villages and places where people don't have a Bible in their language.

I have friends with such strong convictions in spreading the Word of God that they reprint Bibles at their own cost for those in Muslim, Hindu and Communist countries. In fact, they risk their own lives to smuggle them into those countries.

Intrinsic vs. Extrinsic Belief

Approximately 90% of Americans say that they believe in God. However, for many, their faith is rooted in 'cultural' Christianity, not a deep belief in God. Likewise, 75% believe the Bible is the actual Word of God. Yet, most do not know the rules and principles of their faith, which are the foundations of the Bible.

Dr. Ken Cooper, who coined the phrase 'aerobics' and is the author of many bestselling books, says that there are two basic kinds of belief from the scientific point of view. *"The first is extrinsic belief, almost a rote or mechanical affirmation of convictions of spiritual faith. The distinguishing feature of this sort of belief is that it remains in the head and never makes it to the heart. Various studies prove that this type of belief does not improve a person's spiritual status, emotional well-being, or physical health."*

He continues, however, *"Intrinsic belief is characterized by a spiritual commitment to the meaning of life, heartfelt prayer and a quest to be changed. This kind of inner conviction which may be accompanied by, but never limited to, outward, external observance is the key to real spiritual power."* Real spiritual power is rooted in and created by the Word of God.

According to polls of the ABC TV Network, 46% of all Americans say they are born-again Christians. What does that really mean? It means they have submitted their lives to serve God. Many call it a salvation experience. We are first born of the body and of water. Being born again means that we are born of the spirit as we connect with the Lord. The Spirit of God flows into our hearts, and we now have a willingness to be open to Him and His leading. We begin to gain in spiritual knowledge and understanding for our lives. The cobwebs of our mind, or 'stinking thinking,' and soul wounds are reduced and other insights become greater.

Surrendering our will to His will is when He comes in and brings His spirit to help us feel a deeper love beyond our own understanding. As we seek more knowledge and insight, the Lord responds especially during the trials of life causing us to grow in our relationship with Him. Studying His word teaches us His ways and we know how to recognize His voice and ways. We learn to *"abide in Me and I will abide in you."*

From the conversion experience of Paul, the Jew, who wrote so much of the New Testament, he said in Acts 9:18, the *"scales fell from my eyes."* He could then see Jesus in the Spirit.

Chuck Colson also found true-life-real meaning, real purpose, real identity, and real security in coming to know Jesus Christ. Colson was former chief counsel for President Nixon and went to prison because of his participation in the Watergate scandal. He said he lost his 'ego trappings' of limousines, servants, and people fawning over him. By going to prison, he found something much better. His salvation experience gave him real and everlasting peace of mind. To him, those things are deeper and are eternal, much more so than the false gods or temptations of our world.

The frustration for some Christians is that they never get into second gear. They never make a spiritual inner conviction to which Dr. Ken Cooper refers. They may turn to the Bible, but never read it in an earnest way to grasp how the truth applies to their lives.

That happened to John. He missed the depth and full understanding of his walk the first 10 years because he failed to study, understand, and seek the Lord through His Word.   John thought if he just prayed and worked hard, he would achieve His plan. His Christian knowledge came from Church, pastoral teachings and the witness of fellow believers.

One day, he made a bad decision, thinking that he had arrived in his Christian walk. He felt confident he was in His calling so he stopped his pursuit of Biblical study and wisdom.

All his business knowledge came from experts in the field, of whom very few had a sound spiritual faith or biblical understanding. He says, it was the biggest mistakes of his life. Then one day he slipped into a deep depression, which took him seven years to gradually recover by studying and getting into the deepest depth of his calling and purpose. He became whole through learning how to seek God and His leading through the Holy Spirit. John credits Crown Ministry, founded by Howard Dayton, which taught him how to study the word and bring joy to his spiritual walk into the depth of his present calling..

Brig has had similar up and down experiences coming to know the depth of the Lord's word and His calling. Its inspired his life and attitude in being positive in visions and his charismatic nature that has drawn millions of people to follow him in his different businesses. Today, he will spend as much as two hours a day in the Word to find inspiration, peace and joy that sustains his work and life.

A National Heritage

Our founding fathers used the Bible as the guide for our nation and heritage. They passionately stated, *"We don't want to repeat the mistakes of England with a church of state. We don't want monarchs or dictators over this land."* They wanted freedom from the chains of the past. They wanted a society based on free will, which is a gift from God.

Our founding fathers created our judicial system from the book of Judges in the Old Testament. They developed most of our laws from the Ten Commandments. In fact, the Ten Commandments, carved in marble, still sit above the chambers in the Supreme Court. Today some worldly thinkers are attempting to remove the Ten Commandments and any biblical reference from our government, public schools, the political arena, and even our nation's historical landmarks.

Amazing, isn't it? This is a critical and historical time. Scriptures are all over the different buildings in Washington, D.C. The founding fathers put them there with the purpose of reminding us and keeping them in the fabric of our lives. They are there to remind us of our heritage and from where our principles were derived.

We Stake the Whole Future . . .

James Madison, one of the signers of the Constitution and later a President, said, *"We stake the whole future of American civilization not on the power of government . . . far from it. We stake the future of all of our political institutions upon the capacity of each of us and all of us to govern ourselves according to the Ten Commandments of God."*

In other words, the political institutions he is referring to are businesses, governmental agencies, banks, retailers, churches, synagogues, and all other organizations. It is really about a code of conduct of moral truth from the Ten Commandments. How do you treat your neighbor and how does your personal discipline and conduct cause you to act toward others? Our laws are designed for this purpose. Do not steal, lie, murder, bribe, or commit adultery.

In fact, even the law in the early days of the Commonwealth of Massachusetts stated that if someone committed adultery, they were to be put on public display and chained there for days. Finally, the civil liberties union of its day protested. They said, *"We can't keep doing that, we're shaming people."* Or as many would say today, violating their rights.

Our founding fathers sought freedom on our behalf. A freedom never granted to people by kings or governments. God granted these freedoms to man. But in order to create a free society, the founders had to establish boundaries, rules, and self-disciplines. They sought those principles and guidelines that were found in the Bible. That is why they established laws and a culture around the moral truths of the Ten Commandments. At the same time, they knew they could not legislate or require by law that people love God or even love one another. God is a spirit of love. To tell people to love cannot be done by command. It has to be heartfelt to be real.

To internalize love requires a commitment to the Master of Love who uses His Holy Spirit to magnify it. We then demonstrate externally what is done internally.

Three Ways we are Blessed

After years of working with successful entrepreneurs, studying business and the Bible, both of us have concluded that God blesses us in three ways. The death of Christ on the cross allows God to forgive and bless us by His choice. As we follow His principles—whether we know them or not—we will be blessed as long as we are in His calling and grace.

The Lord is giving us visions and ideas to people—whether we know Him or not—giving us a specific assignment to do our part to move the world forward. If we have no spiritual underpinning, we won't know when He is speaking to us. We then think that we just got a good idea from our own creativity, rather than from Him. God chooses to bless us by three ways:

1. **By His Grace**—He blesses and protects us even though we don't deserve it.

2. **By His Principles**—This is why we are more blessed economically than most nations; coming from the principles instilled in our nation by our founding fathers who used the Bible as their guide.

3. **By His Spirit**—He leads us to do common and uncommon things.

Grace Periods End

When people have violated a law there are normally three types of punishment.

1. **Justice**—being convicted of a crime and receiving the full penalty for what you deserve.

2. **Mercy**—being given a lesser punishment for your offense.

3. **Grace**—someone else accepts the punishment for you.

You have seen us discuss how Grace is God's unmerited favor. We don't deserve it. Christ died on the cross for all of us. He accepted the punishment for our sins. Yet, all of us still sin. Instead, of God continuing to accept animal sacrifices for the atonement for their sins, God sent his Son to die on the cross. Before Jesus came mankind made little progress in the world. The favor of Christ has helped all nations move forward.

Anyone with a car or mortgage payment knows what a 'Grace Period' is. The time between when the payment is due and when it must be paid. Normally ten days. It's a legal term used by lawyers in other circumstances, as well. For many people their entire life may seem like one gigantic 'Grace Period'. They die and don't have any significant setbacks.

Sin ultimately stems from being out of the will of God. In a free will society many people carry multiple sins and are afraid to make a change. The consequences of sin—without grace—may be sickness, jail or job loss or even homelessness. Many punishments come violating the laws of the land. Many sins stem from pride, lust, greed, addictions. laziness, jealously and anger—all false gods. Some people on drugs die from overdose while some experience extended Grace to face a turnaround and break the habit.

When Grace seems to have left you—it's often God's signal to change. If you are living in fear and things are getting worse, He is saying turn to Me—*"I will give you rest, if you surrender to me."* If you are about to go bankrupt, He is waiting for you to turn to Him and produce a miracle. Or it could be less dramatic in that God wants you to sell the business and begin a ministry or being willing to pray with your employees.

The Grace Period ends in a thousand different ways when God wants you to make a change and you feel some type of discomfort or leading to make changes. This is why being in His will, listening for His voice is a much more peaceful journey.

The Economic Impact

Bill Bright, founder of Campus Crusade for Christ, a worldwide ministry in the 1990's claimed that the United States have only 5% of the world's population but 54% of its wealth. Today some would say while the population percentage stays virtually the same, the wealth projection is more like 40% because of the growth of Far Eastern economies. It is not easy to measure wealth because it's tied up in the assets of private individuals and corporations. But my research has found that the gross world product (GWP) of the USA is equal to the combined total of the next five nations (Japan, Germany, China, Great Britain, and Canada). In fact, 11 of the top 20 billionaires in the world were Americans in 2011.

So, what makes us so much stronger economically? Because our code of conduct in America is based on a foundation of biblical principles of how we treat our fellowman. Our actions, in alignment with these principles, create economic exchange and financial gain when they're continually repeated with the right character and moral behaviors. Both the customer and the entrepreneur have freedom of choice. When we exchange goods and services honorably with the right values, quality, and follow-through, it is a rewarding experience that we want to duplicate again.

Even our laws are not perfect but good in comparison. They are geared to catch the abusers of the Ten Commandments. Therefore the amount of graft, corruption, or bribery we experience is much less than most underdeveloped nations of the world. Those are some of the keys that determine a nation's economic growth and development. Our country is also compassionate and gives away billions of money and resources. We offer freedom with more abundance and, for the most part, are a praying nation.

Jesus said to love your enemies. As a nation, the United States has been willing to stand for the principles of our founders. We have become the world's peacemaker with the compassion to help nations revive and keep others from creating wars.

> *"We can't live without pain or discomfort.*
> *It tells us when to go to the bathroom, eat, sleep,*
> *study, improve, exercise and try harder.*
> *Pain leads us to good by God's design."*

Love Your Enemies

Through the Marshall Plan in Europe after World War II, we helped rebuild Germany and the countries of our allies. General MacArthur introduced the concept of building cars as a major industry to Japan. With the help of Edward Deming (an American consultant who taught top management how to improve design product quality, testing, and sales including the application of statistical methods), Japan has become one of our biggest competitors. Japanese companies sell more cars in the United States than anywhere else in the world.

The standing chuckle for many years has been for underdeveloped countries to pick a fight with the United States and plan to lose. The United States will then pour in so many resources that you will become a wealthy nation. But there is also another unfortunate strategy that works. Do as North Korea has done. Develop your own nuclear arms, and the USA will pay you billions to get rid of them. In time, Iraq may be a strong country from our efforts.

In the mid 90's, John was asked to speak to hundreds of business executives who had come from former communist nations. When the Iron Curtain came down and communism fell in Eastern Europe, they came by the thousands to the USA to learn about our economic successes.

One troubled young man said, *"I don't understand you Americans. How do you give someone your credit card and trust that they are only going to charge you $20 and not $200? Can you really trust people to be honest? We can't do that. We can't trust anybody."*

Under Communism, there was no trust. You were followed and spied upon when ever the Government decided with the threat of jail or torture. America was built on a system of faith, trust, rights, laws and relationships that many now take for granted. Yes, we are also a nation driven by goals and accomplishments. Most Americans are not really money driven, but are seeking significance through self-achievement. The worldly view of success misleads us from the Father's design.

Ken Blanchard, the noted author, speaker, and consultant says. *"Profits are really the praises of the customer and should not be considered the measure of a company's worth."* We have taken that to extreme through the pressures of Wall Street. The pressure is to be an investor with short-term thinking. It is a driving force contributing to our economic success as a nation, but brings as many curses as blessings if it becomes greed.

CHAPTER 4

The Grand Design for Marketplace Success

It doesn't take long to discover that America was founded (and has operated on) biblical principles. It should also be evident that the success of any life endeavor is dependent on our level of commitment to such principles. Let us look at some specifics as to how to apply these principles in your life to achieve the true success of a millionaire.

First, let's define the word 'secret.' It is a significant, mysterious, and compelling word for most people. Webster's Dictionary says it is information that is kept from public knowledge or hidden. It is exclusive information that is concealed and limited to only a few people.

Everybody is yearning to know *"the secret."* Americans today want to know the secret to weight loss, the secret to having a great family, the secret to great relationships, or the secret to making a lot of money. After researching on Amazon.com, we have found that there are 340,000 books with the word 'secret' in their title.

True Secret

We found the word *"Love"* occurred most frequently in book titles because it is the theme of the majority of songs, novels and the cornerstone of the world for building relationships. Our research showed 417,000, title references for Love—not that far ahead of secret. So, you can see how marketers use the world's infatuation with the word 'secret' to their advantage.

God gave every one of us an appetite and desire for comfort, and the satisfaction of living a good life. Since the world's perspective is most publicized, we are constantly reminded through all forms of advertising of those appealing products and services that will make us happy. And we crave to know the secret of a better life.

We both read and study the Bible every day. Jesus seldom used the word secret in the word. Yet, He refers to the *"Secret of the Kingdom"* which is repeated in three different places: once in the book of Matthew, once in the book of Mark, and again in the book of Luke. Jesus referenced it as the *"Secret to the Kingdom,"* which means the secret to life in God's kingdom in both heaven and earth. (NIV)

In fact, when asked how we should pray, Jesus replied, in Matthew 6:9-11 *"Our Father in heaven, hallowed be your name, your kingdom come, your will be done, on earth as it is in heaven. Give us today our daily bread."*

In other words, His kingdom is ideal and supersedes anything on earth. It trumps our worldly model for success.

He continues that Secret to the Kingdom (true secret to living in this world) is found in the *"Parable of the Sower."* Soon, we will go into depth of the parable. If you can truly grasp its insights and wisdom, you will greatly increase your odds of becoming a true millionaire.

Seeing With Spiritual Eyes

Tapping into the power of the founders' perspective gives us the ability to see as deeply as they did in envisioning the future of our nation. If we can recognize the spiritual plan of the Designer, we start to see beyond the typical worldly thinking, which is caught up in a self-centered life style that focuses on instant gratification and short-term goals.

Like any field general, football coach, or CEO, we have to be able to project into the future, not only the next move, but also many moves ahead. For instance, the game of life is similar to chess. The name of the game is strategy, anticipation, flexibility and being open to His insights and leading using different players with different abilities to make progress.

As spiritual beings living in this world, we need to become bilingual because we have a dual citizenship. Here on earth and in heaven. We must think short term as well as long term. While we live on this earth (short term), we are not of this world, but more importantly citizens of heaven. We also have a long-term destiny and a role to play in the Designer's plan while on earth. As we interact with others and go about our business, our direction and guidance positioning system (GPS) should come from the One who created us and wants us to follow His plan.

When we die, our soul—which is our mind, will and emotions—and spirit—heart and connectivity to God—will go to Heaven.

Our spirit is also referenced in the Bible as our heart, which reaches beyond logic and connects with the Spirit of God. You will start to recognize this as we discuss the parable.

The *"secrets"* are more deeply explained and understood if we tap into our spiritual understanding. Samuel Clemens (Mark Twain) said, *"It ain't what you know that gets you into trouble, but what you know, that ain't so."* The Bible says, *"Abide in me, and I will abide in you."* Our spiritual journey involves opening our eyes to truth, getting to know Him, and allowing Him to work through our personality, talents, and thinking.

Spiritual Discernment

"The man without the spirit does not accept the things that come from the Spirit of God, for they are foolishness to him because he lacks spiritual discernment." 2 Corinthians 2:14 Our openness and

relationship to the Spirit of God affects our ability to know and hear His voice or accept His ways.

Yet, if we haven't made that commitment of surrender to His will, the Spirit of God patiently continues to wait until we are sincere and ready to be in a trusting relationship with Him. Spiritual discernment involves a growing understanding of God and a daily surrender to His will. It is a deepening sincerity of the heart to honor and serve the Lord, and set aside our own agenda. As Chuck Colson puts it, the peace of mind that follows surpasses all understanding.

Do you have a GPS in your automobile? Wherever you go, your GPS helps you navigate through the streets and along the highways to your destination. Once you enter your destination and it locates your position and guides you every step of the way. In fact, if you take a wrong turn, it resets itself with a 'course correction.'

Do you realize that God has a Global Positioning System of His own? In fact, man's version of this came from God. It's called *"God's Positioning System."* He has been using it for centuries by the leading of the Holy Spirit. Throughout the course of history, He has positioned and readjusted men and women. If you are listening closely you will hear the Holy Spirit say, *"Recalculating"* as he gives us another opportunity to exit and get back on course.

When we make mistakes, whether big or small, and get off track, the Lord is there attempting to get our attention and get us back on course. He never gives up on us. It is part of His eternal plan to welcome as many people as possible into His Kingdom. God lets us take detours in life. It's part of free will. What we learn from our mistakes can be used to help others in the long run.

> *"The Visions and Dreams of our imagination is the work of the Holy Spirit."*
>
> PASTOR DAVID YONGGI CHO, PASTOR
> OF THE LARGEST CHURCH IN THE WORLD IN SEOUL, KOREA

Richest Man on Earth

At 33 years of age, John D. Rockefeller, was America's first millionaire. At 43, he ran the largest company in the world, Standard Oil. At 53, he was America's first billionaire. By this time, in the early 1900s, he was so sick that he could only eat crackers and milk. He was on his deathbed. Newspapers had written his obituary. They thought he was going to die. At the same time, he was hung in effigy because people hated him and said he was full of greed.

Rockefeller called himself a Christian, so what happened? Although he realized God had given him the gift to accumulate wealth, the gift had become a curse because he didn't seek or know his true purpose in gathering wealth. This reminds me of a statement a pastor once said about being wealthy, *"God will give it to you, if He can get it through you."*

One night, when he couldn't sleep, Rockefeller sought God and received a vision. He realized in the vision that the Lord was saying, *"All the money in the world will do you no good in heaven or hell. Your job and your responsibility are to give it away."* The next morning he brought his staff together to form the John D. Rockefeller Foundation. His philanthropy has changed the world, set the pattern for other philanthropists, and wiped out many diseases, including malaria during the early part of that century.

So as Rockefeller discovered his true calling, his health turned around and he received the *"peace of mind that surpasses all understanding."* His inner healing led to his outer physical healing. Rather than dying, he spent the next 40 years giving away the wealth he had accumulated.

The Lord spoke these words to me.

> ***"True wealth is not a measure of success***
> ***but of responsibility."***
>
> JOHN BEEHNER

If you have money, talents, or gifts, then helping other people is your greatest responsibility and honor. We all have a responsibility to one another to give away the gifts He has placed within us and to help change lives. His purpose in us is fulfilled as we use these gifts to touch the lives of others. The truth and depth of the secret to living comes alive in you through a spiritual understanding, which becomes deeper and deeper over time. In fact, as you read the Bible repeatedly with spiritual eyes, you are refreshed and enlightened to the true wisdom of God.

Do you remember in high school English class when the teacher asked you to read a poem or a piece of literature? Afterward, the teacher asked, *"What is the author really trying to say? What is his deepest meaning?"* That's what starts to unfold as we begin to see the depth of biblical truth and read between the lines. The true meanings start to come into view, and then it broadens our vision and gives us a greater understanding.

That's the spirit of God at work in you. It is seeing with spiritual eyes, which the Bible also calls our heart. When you see a vision through grace, you begin to understand your calling. This is the track that you are to be on in life in terms of how you are to help people—by being a better father, husband, mother, wife, friend or even building a business, ministry or other enterprise.

God then brings the provision or *"pro-vision."* In other words, you receive the vision and then let God take the lead, but you have to mentally let go. He will then lead while helping you grow and resolve issues by His Spirit and grace.

Life-Changing Experiences

John Beehner surrendered to the Lord in 1981. At that time, he knew very little about the Bible or a personal relationship with the Lord. Within the same week he had a spiritual insight about his struggling business. He trusted the Lord was sending him a message. He had arranged a famous speaker from Dallas to come to speak to his corporate client. The day before the speech he received a call that the speaker was sick but another man was coming in his place. As he hung up the phone, in his spirit he heard that the new man was coming to tell him something about his business. The new speaker flew in from Texas to deliver his speech for John's client, an Insurance corporation with 300 executives in attendance. At lunch, he shared about what he was doing in his business, which was very similar to John's. He also casually shared information about another business that John had never heard of.

As he began to describe this other business, John said, *"My life stopped. I vividly saw six pictures scroll across the screen of my mind. Those mental pictures were places and positions I had held that would prepare me to become a part of the new business he was sharing with me."*

The business was called TEC (The Executive Committee) now known as Vistage. He had never heard of the company, but he knew without a shadow of doubt that he was supposed to be a part of that business. After a few months of negotiating, he started the business. After two years of pioneering the concept, he obtained the rights to offer TEC to CEOs all over the rest of Florida.

The business continued to grow at a healthy pace for 13 years. He had 300 CEOs and executives in the roundtable process in 1994. From the Lord's direction he felt he was called to sell the business and write a book. Within a year the business was sold for more than a million dollars.

A few years later, he had been seeking an investment opportunity. He had prayed and searched for months. Then one night while praying, He heard the still small voice of the Lord saying to contact a gentleman who led him to a piece of property on the ocean. Within a few short years, it became worth a million dollars after only $40,000 down. If you have a discerning spirit, you can recognize the same leading of the Lord.

Seeking God in Business

Seeing the world through spiritual eyes has a dramatic impact on your life, your business, and your relationship with others. Truett Cathy is the founder of Chick-fil-A and a man of strong faith who is open to God's calling and direction. Most of his stores were in malls and shopping centers where he introduced the first chicken sandwich in America. Before the 1980s, the company's sales had been growing by an amazing 15 percent annually.

Yet, in the mid-1980s, his business started to go flat for the first time in it's history. Wendy's, McDonald's and other hamburger chains decided they would also start selling the chicken sandwich. The American public was learning that high cholesterol levels caused by consuming fatty meats were not healthy. During that time, Truett was very concerned and as a result, decided to take his board and some other key company officers away on a two-day planning session to develop a strategic plan for the growth and development of the company.

As the board met, they prayed, talked, and planned, but there was only one key issue that they could really come to agreement over. It was their mission statement: *"We will honor God in all we are entrusted to serve and do."*

From that point on, they placed this statement in front of their corporate headquarters and in the entrances of all their restaurants. In addition, they also honor God by keeping to a company policy to be closed on Sundays. To this day, Truett shares how that meeting was the turning point in the business. After that, 15 to 25 percent annual growth began again. They were doing $500 million at that time. They are now over $3 billion, an increase of billions of dollars in less than 10 years without going public.

Success by Grace

Can you achieve business success without having spiritual eyes? Can you make a million dollars without knowing the founders' plan and the model for our society? Can a loving God still love you when you don't know His ways?

Yes, our Creator has a plan for all of us. We contribute to His plan of moving mankind forward despite our understanding or lack of spiritual eyes. As we said earlier, the Lord still loves the atheist and can use him to build a successful enterprise. But, if you worship the false idols of money, fame, possessions, and power in a start-up business, your chance of survival and success is less. Only 20 percent of all small business start-ups are still in operation after five years. The key is your motive, which leads to focus and future success.

Most mid-size and larger businesses have survived the start-up years by God's grace and following His principles. It is by God's grace that their business is in the right niche, gifting, and calling to serve society even when they have the wrong motives. A number of greedy and egotistical businessmen have discovered their ultimate purpose (often by trial and error). They learn the importance of building relationships and developing obedience without fully understanding how and why they are successful. By following certain steps, processes, or even their gut (heart), they discover how things work.

In other cases, they may have recognized or experienced *"Golden Rule"* role models of their former bosses, suppliers, or vendors. These principles are part of the American fabric established by the founding fathers. However, many businessmen fail to recognize the Lord's direction. Instead, they think they came up with a great idea. God's grace allows for this until the grace period ends.

Through the Lord's GPS system, He is working to achieve goodness through you even when making money is your primary goal. He uses believers and non-believers alike for His purposes. In truth, you do not have to be holy for God to use you. Whether you are in jail or on your 100-foot yacht in the Mediterranean Sea, He uses you for His purposes. If you kill someone or steal, He allows you to fall but patiently waits for you to become remorseful. Even if life is a bumpy ride, His goal for you is to know Him and experience true joy in life.

Can you have peace of mind with $10 million or as an inmate on death row? The answer is yes, if you are sincerely committed to serve Him and knowing Him right where you are. It is a spiritual encounter with God where you find your spiritual eyes.

A Grand Design to Use Us

God can, and does use people like Ted Turner, Bill Gates, Donald Trump, Steve Jobs, and even Bernie Madoff whether they have little or no faith in Him. In the world of high finance, (i.e. stock market, big banks, insurance companies, and investment groups), they are selling personal and financial success. So where does the need for financial growth and greed separate?

Obviously, making money is important to the survival of any business, and it is also a measurement tool for business success. But our worldly perspective in our free society seems to overemphasize the making of money, misleading people away from the foundational principles of success. This fuels the flame for public companies to live and die by their quarterly profit and loss statements. It also perpetuates the greed for money, fame, possessions, and power at the highest levels. So how can businesses be so successful? They can't without first using our founders' principles of purpose, loving relationships, and obedience. Without them, there is no long-term financial success.

The stories of major financial scandals of Bernie Madoff , Enron, Arthur Andersen, Martha Stewart, and Merrill Lynch are just examples of how egotism creates greed, lying, and stealing and can lead to the collapse of major course corrections. This often damages the lives of everyone associated because of the self-centered decisions of a few power hungry leaders.

For instance, the downturn in the housing market was largely fueled by the oversupply of loan money for under-qualified borrowers, known as the subprime market. Major banks and financial institutions wrote down their losses from being over extended, hurting thousands upon thousands of investors and millions of homeowners. This is part of God's design for *"free will."* As we get out of His will or plan we suffer and become more open to His grand design.

Global Prosperity

God's principles apply to four areas of life simultaneously:

1. Individuals

2. Families

3. Organizations

4. Nations

From America's example, influence and leadership nearly three quarters of the nations have declared freedom or some form of democratic process. China is an example of a country declaring economic freedom and backing out of Communism.

Economic exchange occurs when someone is in God's will and uses the right character traits within His calling and morally offers his customers, suppliers, and employee's products or services with integrity. That's the Golden Rule in action. When that practice is performed over and over, it creates growth over the long term, which multiplies his value or equity. Very often, he or she becomes a millionaire.

When liars or cheater do business and promise what they can't or don't intend to deliver, the business cannot last long term, because customer won't continue to do buy their services. Very few will be able to continue, as long as Bernie Madoff did.

From our Designer's perspective, He has a plan to move the world forward, not only in your business of reaching financial goals, but also in nations all over the earth. Many complain that America is sending many jobs overseas. Yet, God is working through this to accomplish His global plan for all mankind.

We are convinced the Lord uses America's economic character and moral strengths to bring the whole world closer to His biblical plan. We are called to export jobs because it is part of His grand plan. He is bringing the world together and creating jobs to have economic opportunities for all people.

In fact, if we believe in a sovereign God, technology and the Internet were visions and plans of God. He gave the ideas and inspiration to individuals and groups to carry them forward. America is a tool and resource for the Lord to bring freedom and opportunity to the world. At the same time, the Lord uses America to spread Christian principles through our economic success.

If employees have not learned the Golden Rule at home, they can learn it in the market place by the way other people treat them with kindness and respect. Hopefully they will take these values home and will treat their families with more kindness and love. For too many, their best family may be at the office or plant.

His grand scheme for jobs is to always move toward cheap labor for poorer countries. Freedom creates the opportunity for competition, which means that man needs to keep finding ways of greater efficiency. When prosperity raises the standard of living in Asia high enough, the cheaper jobs go to Africa. This results in a decline in communism, racism, and poverty.

He is leading us to systematically reach the world with His gospel and provide the opportunity to know Him. In a manner of speaking, the largest mission field and at the same time largest Church in the world—is business. Business in a free society teaches values, procedures, productivity, and communication with respect. Everyone is considered valuable. Although many businesses are not teaching spiritual knowledge, they must teach the other two cornerstones, character and moral principles, or they eventually die.

What does this have to do with you becoming a millionaire? It demonstrates that you are part of a grand plan. So, be ready. If you are not doing business with other nations, get ready. Even if you have already made your first million, you may qualify to receive another vision that leads to a higher calling in business or even a ministry. The true *"secret"* that creates millionaires is about to be revealed.

Reference details on global prosperity in the book, *"The Freedom Revolution—Rocking our World. The inspiring story of how Freedom and the Church are transforming nations."*

Obstacles to Lasting Success

- Lack of knowledge and intimidation.

- Lack of Faith or blind Faith without confirmation.

- Great Vision without clarity or knowing the cost.

- Blind Trust of people without accountability.

- Procrastination or waiting for the pain to become severe enough to have to take action.

- Insecure in my ability or over confident in my ability.

- Fear of Success or Failure—listening to the doubts and negative thoughts of your demons.

- Too comfortable in my old habits to change.

- Price too high vs. my level of trust/confidence with people or products or services.

Conditions of the Soul

Seed visions work to penetrate and grow within us

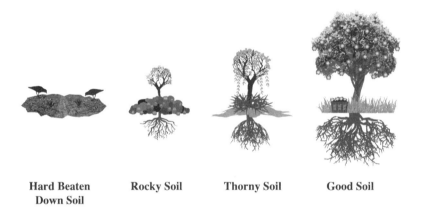

Hard Beaten
Down Soil   Rocky Soil   Thorny Soil   Good Soil

CHAPTER 5

The Secret
of the Soils

In years working with CEOs and executives, hiring motivators and experts, we both recognized one very profound teaching point. You can tell people a principle, but until you illustrate or share an example their ability to envision how it works is limited. They need to understand its application. This is why Jesus spoke so often in parables and the Bible is full of stories about people.

Jesus is quoted as saying, *"the knowledge of the kingdom Kingdom of God has been given to you (meaning committed believers), but to others I speak only in parables so that through seeing they may not see, through hearing, they may not understand."*

Jesus said the secret of the kingdom Kingdom is found in the Parable of the Sower. A parable is a metaphor, story, or an example that dramatizes a principle. Amazingly, Jesus is quoted three times, practically word for word, using the same illustration.

In fact, we can't find another complete parable repeated three times in the Bible! Nowhere else does Jesus use the word *"secret"* in this manner. Each passage describes it as the *"secret to the Kingdom."* So according to the writers of the New Testament, Jesus only used the words *"secret of the Kingdom"* in reference to the Parable of the Sower. This truth must have been so strong and profound that the writers (Matthew, Mark, Luke) allowed it to be repeated three times. Perhaps Jesus repeated it often or the writers saw greater depth and meaning from this parable. This means it was so important that it has an emphatic impact on each of our lives and we should see how it relates to our past, present and future. The Parable of the Sower uses four stories of casting or planting seed on different types of soil.

This parable, as is true for many others, can relate to many areas of life including marriage, friendships, and organizational development. For our purpose, we are using it to reveal *"The Untold Secret that Creates True Wealth."* Hidden within this powerful parable are the truths needed to develop your enterprise and embark on your journey to success.

> *"The Lord shows me enough,*
> *as a lamp upon my feet...*
> *just to take me one step at a time."*
> BRIG HART , CO-FOUNDER OF USAASSOCIATION

The Power of the Seed

Before delving into the Parable of the Sower, we need to reveal insights of Jesus' illustrations of planting seed, especially since very few of us have any farming experience.

In God's design, all life begins as a seed and reproduces after its own kind. The Bible refers to three types of seed.

1. **Natural Seed**— Plants and crops come from physical seed. Planted in the right soil, they reproduce more seed to allow man to continue the cycle of growth. Plants and crops also provide nourishment for man and the soil, as well as clothing and oxygen.

2. **Human (and Animal) Reproductive Seed**—As a male's seed fertilizes a woman's egg, conception begins and new life is created. The more fertile a woman's ovary (soil), at the right cycle of the month, the better chance the sperm has to take root. Just like in plants and crops, new seed produces more of

its own kind. Each generation produces more and inherits from its forefathers. The Bible says the sins and blessings of the father and mother are passed on for 10 generations—not just physical and mental traits, but spiritual as well.

The Bible also refers to the Jews as the seed of our Christian faith, as the sons of Abraham and God's covenant with His people.

3. **Spiritual Seed**—The Spirit of God creates spiritual seed that is manifested in the form of words, visions, and unctions. In the beginning, God spoke the world into existence by the power of His tongue—His seed words. Since we are created in His image, He gave us a remnant of the same power.

Through Him and the spirit of His Word (the Bible), God impregnates us with His plans for our success. However, these plans require that we take risks and remain open to change. The enemy seeks to destroy those plans and wants us to reproduce negativity in our thinking and our influences.

New life from Death

John 12:24 says, *"Very truly I tell you, unless a kernel of wheat falls to the ground and dies, it remains only a single seed. But if it dies, it produces many seeds."*

Two principles here for believers:

1. **A seed represents life.** Each of us are like seeds that must die—to our old ways—by giving up our own will in order to be planted in the garden of Christ's plan and intent in a new life—or new growth cycle—for His purpose.

2. **The seed idea or vision that God gives you won't be successful without your receptivity, openness and embrace.** Yet, a successful business or ministry will multiply and bare much fruit many times over.

Living Words

Words are the living and spiritual seed of life. They are thoughts and containers filled with emotions, meanings, mental pictures, information, and direction. Think of words as the DNA of a seed in our hearts—our spirit. After they are planted, they grow and dictate our emotions and decision-making. Scripture refers to the words on our tongue as a rudder on a ship. With the slightest turn of the rudder, it changes the direction of a huge vessel. The same applies when we use our tongue. It moves the body, soul, and spirit.

Seed words can demean, insult, and start wars. Yet they also bring love, peace, joy, and harmony to our lives. If you were called names in school, chances are your Mom said, *"Sticks and stones may break your bones but words will never hurt you."*

Unfortunately, our mothers probably never really considered the powerful impact of words.

For instance have you ever said to yourself?

"I'm such a loser."

"People don't like me."

"I'll never measure up."

"I'll probably fail"

"I'll never be successful because of _____

(fill in the blank)."

These negative words flash across our heart and soul because the enemy of God wants to deceive us. He wants to keep us neutralized and off track from the Lord's plans. His tactics prevent us from bearing fruit in our lives.

We all carry scars from experiences and negative word seeds. They limit our faith, confidence, and receptivity to new thinking. Ultimately, they hinder our ability to achieve success. In contrast, the Lord uses His seed words to motivate, encourage, and empower us. He does this through the Bible, through principles and truth, through visions, thoughts, and by His messengers.

By empowering us through His living words, God intends to form us into a living image of success. But we have to be willing to die or let go of our 'stinking thinking' fears and anxieties and cast away the old seed words that negatively impact our lives. Don't forget Jesus said, *"unless a kernel of wheat falls to the ground and dies, it remains only a single seed. But if it dies, it produces many seeds."*

The question is, are you willing to die from your plan for achieving success? Are you willing to open your heart to real truth? The path to real success can be found in the secret message in the Parable of the Sower.

The Parable of the Sower

"A farmer went out to sow his seed. As he was scattering the seed, some fell along the path, and the birds came and ate it up. Some fell on rocky places, where it did not have much soil. It sprang up quickly, because the soil was shallow. But when the sun came up, the plants were scorched, and they withered because they had no root. Other seed fell among thorns, which grew up and choked the plants. Still other seed fell on good soil, where it produced a crop—a hundred, sixty or thirty times what was sown. Whoever has ears, let them hear."

The disciples came to him and asked, *"Why do you speak to the people in parables?"*

He replied, *"Because the knowledge of the secrets of the Kingdom of heaven has been given to you, but not to them. Whoever has will be given more, and they will have abundance. Whoever does not have, even what they have will be taken from them. This is why I speak to them in parables:*

"Though seeing, they do not see; though hearing, they do not hear or understand."

In them is fulfilled the prophecy of Isaiah:

> *"You will be ever hearing but never understanding;*
> *you will be ever seeing but never perceiving.*
> *For this people's heart has become calloused;*
> *they hardly hear with their ears,*
> *and they have closed their eyes.*
> *Otherwise they might see with their eyes,*
> *hear with their ears,*
> *understand with their hearts*
> *and turn, and I would heal them."*

"But blessed are your eyes because they see, and your ears because they hear. For truly I tell you, many prophets and righteous people longed to see what you see but did not see it, and to hear what you hear but did not hear it.

"Listen then to what the Parable of the Sower means:

"When anyone hears the message about the kingdom and does not understand it, the evil one comes and snatches away what was sown in their heart. This is the seed sown along the path.

"The seed falling on rocky ground refers to someone who hears the word and at once receives it with joy. But since they have no root, they last only a short time. When trouble or persecution comes because of the word, they quickly fall away.

"The seed falling among the thorns refers to someone who hears the word, but the worries of this life and the deceitfulness of wealth choke the word, making it unfruitful.

"But the seed falling on good soil refers to someone who hears the word and understands it. This is the one who produces a crop, yielding a hundred, sixty or thirty times what was sown."

- MATTHEW 13:1-23

Seed Capital

We find it ironic that when Jesus spoke of the 'seed.' (Vision. Ideas, Unctions or Leadings of the Lord) that He places in the hearts and souls of individuals to take a risk with a new idea. Financial investors who offer initial investment capital as 'Seed Capital or Angel Capital' use similar terminology. Did they get their vocabulary from the Bible or was it the Holy Spirit speaking to their heart with a vision to help others to create their business? As a point of interest, Biblegateway.com says there are 83 references to the word "seed" in the Bible.

CHAPTER 6

The Beaten Down Path

Jesus opens with the parable with the farmer who sows his seed on a beaten down path or barren soil. He says the birds and even the devil came to steal the seed so it has no chance to take root. This is the path that is worn and hard. The seed has no opportunity to begin to take hold.

THORNY SOIL

Hardheaded from hard soil.
Visions often rejected.

Later in the parable, Jesus explains that the soil represents our heart and soul. In this case, the soil of our soul is not fertile. *"When anyone hears the message about the Kingdom and does not understand it, the evil one comes and snatches away what was sown in their heart. This is the seed sown along the path."*

Whenever God sows the seed with His words, vision, or message, He wants to plant and grow it in our heart and soul. The word may be in the form of a new idea, a challenge, or even an opportunity. It can be an invention or a way to solve a problem, a message about our marriage, a message for raising kids, helping relatives, or even our enemies. It represents something to move us closer to our God-given purpose.

When our heart and soul are full of negatives we are beat down with worthlessness. We naturally see obstacles in nearly every idea or vision rather than the potential for growth. Thus, we reject it immediately. The negative seed words that have already taken root, have taken control of our heart and soul.

I once heard a multi-millionaire, talk about how his family had beat into him, some of these words:

- *"Don't go into that business because you don't know enough about it."*

- *"Don't you know where we came from?"*

- *"We've been a family living on welfare most of our lives."*

- *"You can't start a business, you are not smart enough"*

- *"Don't you realize you're not going to be successful?"*

- *"The risk is too big."*

Many in our society have a scarcity mindset rather than faith in prosperity. The doubts from their families keep their mindset in the beaten down soil, making them unreceptive to risk and God's leading.

> **"Change is hard to live with,
> but it's impossible
> to live without."**
> BRIG HART, CO-FOUNDER OF THE USA ASSOCIATION

Knowing the Father's Love

In my early years, of growing up (they called me Brig after my middle name) in the Hart household I lived in a stressful and dysfunctional family. My hurting father turned to alcohol as his medicine but it created all kinds of stress and havoc on all of us. That experience took a deep toll on my inner spirit with many scars. So at 13, I could not take it any more and left to move in with friends and their families until I completed High School.

With hurt and anger in my heart, I was often in trouble and eventually got caught up in drugs. Two years in the Marine Corps straightened me out for a while. The failing years of the surf shops that my brother Dave and I had created, brought me to bouts of depression. I felt like a loser because I even failed twice at committing suicide.

But a business man named Doug saw something in me to persistently pursue me for a business opportunity that changed my life forever. He started his meeting by reading to a group of us one of the most heart warming readings I had ever heard about Love. I asked him, *"who wrote that?"* He said I will introduce him to you and that is how I came to submit my life to Jesus Christ. The business opportunity was a direct selling company known as Am Way which I learned to build for 20 years at the highest level.

What I later came to realize was that God was touching my *"beaten down soul"* with His *"seed"* words of unconditional love and the business opportunity was secondary.

What changed my desperate soul, was the peace, love and joy I experienced from the Lord. That allowed me to begin healing and pass on my *"new heart"* through my business platform, using the gifts I received to inspire hundreds of thousands of others to take a risk to use their gifts and talents with us.

Direct selling is really what I call *"Relationship Marketing"* and was my ministry tool far more than my business. The opportunity to make money, make a living or even gather wealth was just another motivator for people to reach out and find the talents they never knew they had. It became my calling, which I needed to do whether there was lot of money involved or not.

"If you are afraid of failure you will never try success, If you are afraid of success you do not deserve to succeed."

NIDO QUEBIN, PRESIDENT OF HIGH POINT UNIVERSITY

Soul Wounds

Katie Souza, helped us understand best what keeps many people close minded and trapped in the fear of the *"Beaten down path"* resistant to the seed visions the Lord is using to penetrate our soul. Katie, was a former drug pusher who had a dramatic life change in prison through the leading of the Holy Spirit. She believes that she received revelations that address our past scars and fears. She calls them soul wounds (others may call Strongholds) which affect or even grip our subconscious mind. These emotional pains grip us with fear and prevent us from taking risk when we sense the nudging of God. These wounds impact our business and our relationships, our families, our job, our ministry, and our lives. Satan, the evil spirit works to remind every one of these weaknesses, to inhibit us.

Paul may have said it best in Romans 7. *"I do the things I don't want to do because of the sin that lives within me."* Another way of saying it is, *"I just seem to shoot myself in the foot."* When your soul is a beaten down path where the birds and devil come to take away your seed, you don't have the courage to take risks and move forward with any vision.

We all have a body, soul, and spirit, but many of us do not know the distinction between soul and spirit. The spirit is the part of us that has a personal connection with the Lord Himself. If we are willing to trust Him with our lives and ask forgiveness for our sins, then He will lead us and ignite our spirit with His Spirit.

When this happens, you begin to see things that you couldn't fully understand before your spirit was awakened—amazing truths about God, life, and people. It is an exciting journey even though there are still potholes along the road and lots of sacrifices, just as Jesus faced. The Bible often refers to the spirit as our heart—not physical—and the place where His love is received and given.

In contrast, the soul describes the part of us where our will, emotions, mind, and intellect work together. In the midst of this, a great part of our memory lives and records our mistakes, sins, and regrets. These are the things you did to others or they did to you. Add to that mix those traits that are inherited by our parents and ancestors. After all, if we can inherit physical and mental traits, why not *"the sins of the fathers passed down for generations."*

This soul 'soup' can be small or large. Either way, the soul issues inhibit our actions or drive our behavior. It's amazing that even Hollywood talk shows refer to people as 'dealing with their demons,' referring to addictive behaviors or a sinful lifestyle. In fact, they discuss it even more than a typical church.

Your parents, teachers, or school may have berated you with words like, *"You are no good. Or you will never amount to anything."* Others have experienced terrible soul wounds from physical beatings, rape, or molestation. The list can get very long. Even soul wounds that are considered to be small leave scars or 'barnacles' that impact our lives. They take root in our soul and condemn us. Yet the Bible says, *"there is no condemnation in Christ Jesus."*

The fear of risk is directly tied to our soul wounds, these 'barnacles' that prevent us from stepping out of our comfort zone. Still, they do not prevent the Lord from testing you and giving you 'seed opportunities' that could change your life and those around you. In fact, if your mind is telling you, *"you will never amount to anything,"* then the fear of success is very real to you.

> *"Hurting people...*
> *Hurt people.*
> *When people hold onto grudges*
> *they subconsciously rehash them*
> *in their mind and it keeps them from*
> *God's grace and deeper calling."*

Satan's Dirty Little Secrets

Pastor Steve Foss has studied and prayed over how the enemy called Satan tries to beat us down through our weaknesses, scars or soul wounds. Some Pastors say there can be as many as 35-50 different Strongholds that the enemy uses to create fear or turmoil in us through our mind and thinking. Strongholds like pride, fear, addictions, jealousy, lust, depression, abandonment, anger and many more that can influence us. We will mention more as they are connected to the sins of the heart.

But Steve Foss feels the Lord has revealed to him that there are two main stream from which these wounds or strongholds come from...

1. The feeling of Insecurity

2. The feeling of Inferiority

We can all relate to these areas because we are all raised without the Lord until we accept or commit to live for Him. Without Him we have all felt insecure about trying some things or taking risks in areas where we don't feel adequate or inferior to other people.

My calling to write

In 1995, John knew in his heart he was being called by a vision from the Lord to write a book. But out of the fear and wounds in his soul, he told the Lord, *"I can't write a book—a chapter maybe!"*

His soul was reminding me, *"you seldom read books cover to cover, you can barely type—you got a 'D'in high school typing, you don't have a computer and don't have the patience to do the research."* Yet he didn't completely ignore the vision, it stayed in his heart. Being used to delegating, he hired a ghostwriter. When in a few weeks, he knew he had made a mistake. So he tried to research and write on his own. Back and forth, he felt very insecure and unqualified. But after more research, Bible study and prayer he felt he had uncovered some principles of the book. Yet, with more insecurities and thinking that he could not do it, he sought another ghostwriter. He said, *"What I discovered in that up and down journey was that I was battling my own insecurities—the fear of looking stupid and unprofessional."*

He later realized that he also had a 'fear of success.' He had hired 350 speakers a year in his business and saw their life on planes and in hotel rooms, most of the time. He did not want that lifestyle.

Fortunately, the Lord knew better and was not willing to give up on John. He confronted his fears and trusted the Lord to carry him through rather than focus on his inadequacies. He said, *"I told the Lord, I give up and will write this book if you will guide me."* Today this is John's third book and each one is an adventure. Reality is—the person who learns the most from books is not the reader but the author.

Overcoming Discouragement

Discouragement comes from all sides—other people, past failures, and negative thoughts that demoralize us. Satan speaks to our minds and uses the garbage we have collected from negative experiences to tell us how we will fail. He wants us to fail or be handcuffed, thus avoiding God's real call and plan for our lives. People, life experiences and religions, have influenced us all besides institutions that restrict our absorption of the good seed that the Lord is attempting to share with us.

Paul Orfalea really struggled as a kid. He failed two grades and was told he had dyslexia and attention deficit disorder (ADD). We might imagine what people and teachers said. For some parents, this diagnosis may have been heartbreaking, but Paul's parents continued to believe in him. So, when he finally graduated from college, his parents loaned him the $5,000 he needed to start his own tiny copy store near the UC Santa Barbara. You can just hear the negative voices he had heard. Somehow, he persevered and over the next

30 years built Kinko's, a national chain of stores that was eventually purchased by Federal Express.

> *"You can't let your human logic*
> *over ride the Holy Spirit."*
> — SCOTT ADAMS, CPA

Improving Your Emotional Health

Both for children and adults, we are talking about our ability to absorb the good seed sent into our lives. For example, both Brig and John choose to take vitamins while others take prescription drugs. At times, we take more supplements to deal with illnesses or issues. We both have discovered if our intestinal track is cleaner and detoxified, absorption of nutrients and vitamins is much higher.

It is similar to cholesterol build-up in your arteries. When plaque builds up in the inner walls, blood flow is restricted and clogs occur. At the same time, the lining of those arteries can't receive the nutrients from your food carried by your blood. A clean sponge and a clean air filter work the same way.

If you are in pursuit of the wealth journey but have a heart and soul filled with clogged arteries or toxicity, you are probably repelling seed ideas that the Lord wants to birth in you.

Dr. Neil Clark Warren, founder of eHarmony.com®, has saved many marriages from divorce. Through years of counseling and research, he discovered that there are two keys to a successful marriage: emotional health and compatibility. If the emotional health of our soul is stiff and resistant, it is a sign of hard soil in your heart. With God's great love and Grace, He may keep trying to give you His vision, until He will finally find more open individuals to share His visions with. In other words, if your emotional health is good, it gives you strength and resilience through adversity. It keeps you open to new ideas, new people, and the willingness to take more risk.

One of the big business trends over the last decade is to focus on their employee's emotional intelligence, their EQ (Emotional Quotient). It is based in psychology and organizational research. Our EQ relates to how emotionally stable or grounded we are at handling stress on the job. Some say that it determines who will be a 'peak performer' for the organization.

Like eHarmony.com® does through profiling to match applicants with possible soul mates, companies are testing EQ matches before they offer a candidate a new position. In fact, they reject applicants they believe aren't compatible. Do you have hard soil and reject the Lord's attempts to penetrate your heart, build something great, or meet new people who can influence you for change?

Finding Openness

In his early business career in the late 1960s, John chased success because he felt unfulfilled and emotionally hurt. He had a deep longing for inner satisfaction that he couldn't find in running a small Chamber of Commerce. He thought he needed a bigger challenge in a bigger city. So, he started to confidentially talk to different executives about possible positions. At a convention, he met Jerry Bartels, a sharp executive who ran a major Chamber of Commerce in South Carolina. They talked, and he wanted John to come down from Illinois and visit him.

As he later thought about it, he dropped the notion. Why ? When he thought about South Carolina, and Senator Strom Thurmond who had a slow, redneck way of speaking represented his impression. He imagined most people in the same mold, even though he had never been there. This was the 1970s, and he thought people in the South were prejudiced. After all, he was raised in metropolitan Chicago where he associated with very few minorities and saw no prejudice around him. Basically, his heart was hard. He had hard and unreceptive soil.

But God had a plan for him. Five years later, after working for a major company and starting and failing in a small business start up in Maryland, it was time to leave and continue my search for greener pastures.

Amazingly, Jerry Bartels still had an interest in him. So he ended up working for Jerry in Greenville, South Carolina for a few delightful years. He met and worked with wonderful people who had less prejudice than he had experienced in the Midwest. The emotional soil of his heart and soul were too hard the first time, but he was thankful the Lord gave him a second opportunity. At God's initial leading; he was too immature and filled with false impressions to recognize His prompting. This was just part of the Lord's plan to see if he was ready to receive His True Wealth vision and the amazing ride that has taken place since.

> ### *"God meets us at*
> ### *our point of weakness"*
> —EDNA HARRISON HARLIN

Learning from Stubbornness

In the 1990's John Smith, was a young and incredibly successful entrepreneur, at age 28, under God's grace. He had built a chain of 16 athletic shoe stores in malls throughout the Southeast. During the height of his business growth, each store was averaging nearly $2 million in sales per year. John had skipped over some rough paths in life and deep down thought he was smarter than most CEOs.

But the marketplace began to change. His profit margins started to fall, because stores like Wal-Mart and K-Mart were now carrying the same merchandise, Nike and Reebok. Since John was a great athlete in college, his competitive instincts took over. Unfortunately, he refused to listen to several good advisors and the wise counsel he sought. As a Christian, he could not imagine that God would allow what he had built to fail. He developed a new plan to double the number of stores and tried to raise millions of dollars. The 'good seed' was the advice that others had given him. His refusal to listen was due to the condition of his soul.

As things got worse, he had a chance to sell the remaining stores for more than $2 million dollars but said, *"No way."* When he had to close more stores, he had another offer but refused. Finally, he was forced to shut down, owing nearly a million dollars. Pride and stubbornness makes very hard soil. However, after closing the stores, humility became his friend.

The Lord is sending signals if our antenna is up or we are tuned to the right frequency. If God can't plant the seed in the soil of our hard heads and hearts, the grace period over us will end.

Since the years have passed, John has confessed that he wished he had not had such sky rocketing success right out of college. Instead, he would have liked to be able to learn like normal leaders through the typical difficulties and cycles of success and failures. Then he would have been better prepared to handle the decline of his business.

> *"The only thing worse than failure*
> *is not trying."*
> UNKNOWN

Knowing When to Get Help

You may have heard the classic story about the man who had incredible faith in God. During a terrible flood, he believed that God would save him, his home, and his belongings.

When the rains and floods came, he had to get onto the roof of his house. People came by in rowboat and said, *"Get in! It's going to get worse. Save yourself."*

He replied, *"Go on, I will be ok, because the Lord will save me and my home."*

Still, the rain and flooding increased until the water was touching his roofline. Another man in a motorboat came by and said, *"Get in! We can save you."*

But the man on the roof said, *"Go on! The Lord will protect me."* Once again, the waters rose higher. When a helicopter came by and dropped a rope, he refused to take it and yelled that the Lord would save him. In the end, he drowned.

When he got to heaven, he said to the Lord, *"What happened? Why didn't you save me?"*

The Lord said, *"I did try to save you. I answered your prayers by sending two boats and a helicopter."*

Opening our hearts and ears to the advice of others is critical in this journey toward success. The Bible says, *"In this world you will have trouble. But take heart! I have overcome the world."* John 16:33 By trusting in God and watching how He moves in leading our life and help from those who care.

> **"Without counsel, plans go awry,**
> **but in the multitude of counselors**
> **they are established."**
> — PROVERBS 15:22 NKJ

The Hard Way to Learn

Charlie Nesbit was a wonderful man who bought out a family business, which became a leading design-build construction firm. In the 1980s, he was leader in his niche, with a gross annual volume of close to $50 million. Charlie was one of the nicest men any one could ever meet, and he did some very shrewd things in hiring outstanding people. Unfortunately, he got a little greedy, and after nearly 10 years, his key people left to start a competing firm.

When this happened, he believed that it was too late to change course and do something about it. But very determined, he looked at his options and decided he would acquire a smaller firm in trouble. However, he would keep the talented founder of the company because he felt that he would bring in more staff and projects.

As an advisor, he and John talked one on one each month. We also met together with 12 other CEOs that helped each other in business decision-making, a type of Wise Counsel group for secular companies. I said to Charlie before one of the meetings, *"Why don't we bring your planned acquisition to the group for their insights?"*

He said, *"That's not necessary. I've already checked this company out. The founder is a good communicator and we fit well together."*

Even though John had heard of the other company, he thought we should double check and get confirmation from a group of objective outsiders. Something didn't seem right in my spirit. So, I pressured him six times to double check the group, but he refused to share his decision. Within two years, Charlie was out of business. In a private conversation with the other members of the group, John found out three of them knew the entrepreneur Charlie decided to acquire. They said, "That guy is a con man!" In the end, Charlie finally discovered the truth, but it was too late to reverse his deal. In Charlie's case, he didn't want to hear any negatives. He had been hurt and did not want to be hurt again, so he closed the door of his heart to outsiders.

Sometimes we are blind sided by our mistakes and lose objectivity. If we are listening, God is sending messengers. We all have blind spots and consciously or subconsciously put up façades. Other times, our ego gets in the way. That's one reason John is still involved with Wise Counsel. There are times I don't know the answer or others don't know the answer. When we pray together, God knows the answer, and many times, He reveals it to us through others.

Are We Open to Change?

Hard and barren soil relates directly to closed thinking. It's hard-headed thinking and lack of receptivity that prevents good ideas from taking root. We are given ideas and visions, but drop them because of a skeptical heart. Some say, *"been there, done that"* or *"I don't plan to repeat that mistake."* This is where spiritual eyes come into play.

John's good friend. Steve Hall, who leads a ministry for businesses that provide corporate chaplains, talked with me about a recent
meeting. The leader was asking for a volunteer to take on a special
task. Steve said he felt the nudging of the Holy Spirit telling him to
volunteer. The leader was very appreciative.

Later, Steve was praying and thanking the Lord for the opportunity
to take on this task. He said the Holy Spirit said to him, *"You are the
fifth person I have asked."* I am certain we have all turned God down
without really knowing. Do you have a listening heart to hear the call
and the voice of the Lord?

Take the risk and ask God to reveal to you what you need to know
about the risks He wants you take. Test Him. Will he show you?
Learn how to hear His voice or thoughts for you. He will love your
attitude and heart and will not deny your desire.

Franchising Success

The journey to success for McDonald's and Starbucks has some
amazing similarities. Ray Kroc sold milk shake mixers in the 1950s
and was struggling when drug stores—his biggest customers—started to go to self serve and drop their fountain business. Humble and
searching, he had read about the McDonald brothers in San Bernardino, California selling 20,000 shakes per month. He decided
to take the risk and visit them all the way from Chicago. He thought
that if he could convince them to open more stores, he could supply
all their mixers and really grow his business.

When he arrived, he spent the morning observing their operation
from the parking lot. The restaurant had dropped their carhop service because people were willing to stand in line at lunchtime to buy
the 15-cent hamburgers, fries, and shakes. He saw the vision for
thousands of locations around the country.

After the crowd cleared, Ray introduced himself and said, *"My God,
I must get involved with you."* He encouraged the McDonald broth-

ers to franchise. Unfortunately, they felt they had already failed attempting to do that and were resolved to avoid the risk. New changes were not on their radar screen. But after being persistent for a few months, Ray convinced them to be their franchise agent and opened a store in Des Plaines, Illinois to demonstrate to them the vision he could see. The rest is history.

> *"Your problems are not there to*
> *defeat you but to increase you"*
>
> JOEL OSTEEN, PASTOR LAKEWOOD FELLOWSHIP CHURCH

Leveraging a Vision

In 1981, Howard Schultz was general manager of a Swedish kitchen house wares business in New York. He noticed that a small company in Seattle by the name of Starbucks was ordering more coffeemakers than Macy's department store. Howard was intrigued and decided to pay them a visit. At the time, Starbucks had three partners and saw themselves only as coffee importers and roasters. They told Howard *"We don't manage the business to maximize anything other than the quality of the coffee."*

Howard just knew in his heart—seed faith—that he wanted to work in their business and finally convinced them to hire him as director of marketing. He had the burning desire in his heart to accomplish something big. While the partners appreciated Howard's enthusiasm, they had many excuses for not taking the marketing risks he suggested. But within a year, they sent Howard off to a kitchen house wares trade show in Milan, Italy.

While there, he could not help but notice many local coffee shops and how friendly, engaging, and romantic the atmosphere with people who loved coffee. Howard said he saw a vision for coffee shops all over the United States and beyond. But again, the partners were too busy, too entrenched, and too conservative to take a risk on his ideas. Still, they finally let him experiment in one corner of one of there three stores.

With good and consistent results, they still balked at Howard's dreams. Finally, Howard decided to leave and try some shops on his own. Yet one partner, Jerry Baldwin, invested with him in his first store. Howard raised capital and started Il Giornale as an authentic Italian coffee shop. Three stores later, the Starbuck partners decided to sell Starbucks coffee brewing business and name. Howard's board agreed that they needed to buy Starbucks as a long-term growth strategy.

So here's the point to these incredible stories: Both the McDonald brothers and the Starbucks partners had beaten down hearts and were reluctant to take new risk. Some would say those were incredibly big mistakes or missed opportunities. Was the Lord sending them signals or were they not called to be the operators of their original callings?

If you have been approached about a business opportunity or the expansion of your business, where is your heart? Are you open? Do you have all the answers? Is your heart hard or beaten down?

Jump In

Mark Burnett, producer of the The Bible—the big hit TV series on the History Channel almost out drew American Idol. Mark is also producer of Survivor, The Voice, Shark Tank and many other successful TV series, and says that *"many people have ideas. For a believer it's a call of God. For non-believer it's an instinctual call. The question is who will move forward and take the risk? No one likes to fail. If you are not willing to fail—you won't take the risk. If you have Faith in your God or at least yourself, you need to just 'jump in.'"*

He continues, *"I won't spend time around people who dwell on negative thinking. They try to drain my energy from my staff and me."*

Mark took the risk of coming to the USA after years in the British Military. His first job in Los Angeles was being a 'nanny.' Then he started a T-Shirt company before acquiring the right to an Adventure Challenge contest, which eventually opened the door for The Survivor.

Romans 12:2

"Do not conform to the pattern of this world,
but be transformed by the renewing of your mind.
Then you will be able to test and approve what
God's will is—his good, pleasing and perfect will."

Skipping the beat down path

Bill Gates, Paul Zuckerberg and Steve Jobs have had some important and similar traits growing up and maturing in business.

For example, Bill and close friend Paul Allen in high school discovered ways to steal computer time from Computer Center Corporation (CCC). When they were caught Lakeside High School banned them for the summer. Bill discovered a way to exploit bugs in the operating system to obtain free computer time. CCC then turned the tables and found a way to use his talents to improve their system. That was one of Bill Gates first 'research projects' before heading to Harvard. Yet within a few years, he left Harvard hungry to make the practical computer applications for government and business. He and Paul created their own software company beginning with an assignment in New Mexico. Soon after, IBM became one of his major customers, which launched Microsoft in the PC market.

In 2003, Mark Zuckerberg and some fellow Harvard students took some risk by breaking into the University's security network to capture student ID photo's to populate his newly created website called Facemash. Harvard had no student directory and has never been noted as the most 'social' campus on the East Coast. But today, Facebook has celebrated one billion users.

In 1976, Steve Jobs and Steve Wozniak developed the Apple I computer in the garage of his parents. As a teenager, Steve needed parts for a school lab project to develop a frequency counter for computers. He used that as an excuse to call Bill Hewlett, CEO of Hewlett Packard at home seeking spare parts for his project. Bill was surprised but appreciated his boldness and also gave Steve a summer job to learn first hand how computers were assembled.

All three dropped out of college, too busy, too smart and too innovative to waste time getting a degree. But that's OK because all three have earned many honorary degrees. The message here is that God will select many people who are gifted with open soil—open minds— and abrasive thinking that they are too smart to fail. God's seed can connect with their imagination and they have guts to take risks that most people can't fathom.

The common trait within these men was that they were abrasive, aloof personalities and blindly determined. Steve Jobs was fired. Bill Gates was allusiveness through anti trust litigation and Paul Zuckerberg not getting along with others who claimed to help him get started. Jobs and Gates have witnesses to their harsh and sometimes ugly management style and treatment of people at least in their early years. If they had been exposed to this book at that age and time they would have trashed the notion there are cycles and pattern that most business leaders face to find their ultimate success.

God can choose when and He can use who. As you move forward in this book, you will see the tougher soils that these men faced later in the their business journey that changed their lives.

Hard Soil is Short Sightedness
God's plans revealed but hidden to blind eyes and deaf ears

CHAPTER 7

The Rocky Soil

In the next example, the farmer cast his seed amongst the gravel and the rocks. The seeds sprout, but the roots cannot grow enough to become strong, because they are limited by the infertile soil. It is in the rocky places that we limit our long-term receptivity and struggle to allow God's seed to reach deep into our hearts.

ROCKY SOIL

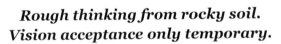

***Rough thinking from rocky soil.
Vision acceptance only temporary.***

In the parable, Jesus said, *"The seed falling on rocky ground refers to someone who hears the word and at once receives it with joy. But since they have no root, they last only a short time. When trouble or persecution comes because of the word, they quickly fall away."*

We may sabotage the vision or literally control our enthusiasm because of a lack of faith. We don't hunger long enough, plan enough, or work hard enough to develop the idea or take more risk. We may become resistant to the change necessary to establish deep roots. We may not have enough belief in ourselves. We may see too much competition or too many problems to overcome, so we give up. It could be that our pride says, *"I'm not willing to sacrifice anything to venture forward anymore."* Our 'stinking thinking,' our souls wounds, and negative seed words eat away at our shallow roots.

Did Jesus mean that the rocky soil in our heart is represented by our sins, mistakes, or bad choices? Do we still own those mistakes because we can't ask for forgiveness? Could they be manifested in how we treat or terminate people? Perhaps, it shows itself in how we fail to plan and how we handle our finances. Do we fail to pay bills on time? Or do we tell white lies about our delivery dates or quality?

Being in the midst of rocky soil can mean you choose the wrong business or even the wrong location. John did that. In the 1970s, he was long on guts and short on wisdom. He started his first business from a dream with enthusiasm for a concept that only lasted 18 months.

In his mind, he was going to be very smart. He thought he prepared himself well. In fact, he spent a year in research with an accountant and hired people with experience as he kept his corporate job. Within the first year, the business did well in gross sales but lost significant money. He had to leave his job, let some people go, and try to build it on his own without the talent and knowledge he needed. His wife told him not to do it, which made him mad. Out of pride he was even more determined to make it work. Thank God, his wife forgave him, rolled up her sleeves, and really tried to help him to keep it alive before he had to close.

A poor business choice, lack of talent, or the wrong calling can place you in the center of the rocky soil. A large number of failures in business start-ups occur in rocky soil. If the rocks of debt don't crush you, it may be ignorance or lack of wisdom.

Was the Lord calling John into that business? No, he doesn't believe so. He believes it was his impatient passion to build something. He had no patience, spiritual understanding, or even knowledge of any type of calling. His mom always said as a kid that he had ants in his pants.

*"In my heart, I had a void
that could only be filled by knowing Him."*

BRIG HART, CO-FOUNDER OF USA ASSOCIATION

John had a personal dream, but looking back, he can't call it a vision. Does the Lord allow us to make free-will mistakes? Of course! Why? Because He can and will use those experiences to teach and prepare us for many other opportunities. It also helps others avoid mistakes and overcome the rocky soil in their lives.

Persistence Leads to Success

You may have heard of Jack Stack. Jack is CEO of SRC (Springfield Remanufacturing Company) in Springfield, Missouri. He has authored several books and the first one is titled the Great Game of Business. Jack and a team of local executives bought the company from the parent owner, International Harvester, a few years before the company finally went bankrupt.

Jack and his team didn't really know what they were doing but had a vision and a desire to keep their jobs. They mustered together about $100,000 and were turned down by 51 banks. How about that for persistence? Finally, the 52nd bank loaned them the money in what many have called the greatest leveraged buyout in U.S. history, a 90 to 1 debt to equity ratio. Now, we would call that rocky soil!

When you are paying 22 percent interest, you've got to scramble. So, they made nearly all their 100 employees owners and taught everyone how to read a financial statement. They met weekly in department meetings and reviewed their P&L statement, projections, and analyzed their cash flow.

Everyone got an incentive plan. Everyone got in on the incentive plan. Every employee was made a stockholder. They ended up creating what is known today as Open Book Management and have grown 20 times. They took the rocky soil and created many divisions in what we believe is an outstanding biblical model for running a successful business. Very similar to what Paul Orfalea did in building Kinko's into a $2 billion dollar business before selling to Federal Express. For innovators that are not willing to quit, rocky soil brings out the best. It cracks open heart and soul to receive new visions required to survive and thrive.

"There is a time to build and a time to uproot, but always holding onto your integrity and the peace of God."

BRIG HART, CO-FOUNDER OF THE USA ASSOCIATION

A future in Rocky soil ?

Brig says, In my early years of direct selling with AmWay, or as I like to call it *"Relationship Marketing,"* I did well in comparison to most other people. The drop out rate was 50%, extremely high after just three months. That and the method of getting people to come to meetings, product delivery, lack of training and the persistence it required to get people to show up, wore on us.

So we pulled back some of our involvement, it really seemed like rocky soil to me. As a result, I started 7 others businesses, i.e. window tinting, building and selling portable storage, towing, custom home building, landscaping and helping our surf shop with my brother. I was just restless and trying to find something better. Those efforts teetered up and down but the direct selling business kept steady as we took in nearly a hundred thousand a year.

I had hired good people in those small businesses but I was overextended and in pure frustration. So my wife Lita and I sought *"wise counsel"* from our Pastor Paul Zink. As Paul looked at our situation and prayed with us, he urged us to concentrate on Amway and step away from other distractions. He had been at some of our conferences and saw how the Lord was using me to motivate and help people to come to Christ...which was the greatest fruit.

I was upset at his advice. But as Lita and I complained to the Lord in prayer, we received more peace about Paul's advice. So we stepped away from the other businesses and committed more deeply to our ministry in direct selling. We pursued through the rocky soil and it paid off handsomely.

Finding the Cure

Dr. Neil Clark Warren faced rocky soil three years into launching eHarmony.com. There had been plenty of men subscribers but not enough women. They faced tough choices; they could have returned all the venture capital and money from subscribers, if they just closed the business down. Instead, they persevered and put more money into television and other media in an attempt to attract more women. They stuck with it, and the rest of the story is history. Today, they have 5 million subscribers, adding 15,000 a day and boasting 33,000 marriages.

Failure leads to Success

Brig Hart, my co-author and friend has had more than a million people in his *"down lines"* after nearly 30 years with Amway and then MonaVie, both Multi-level Marketing businesses. Many don't see MLM as a normal businesses. They are correct, it is not normal. But they are significant training grounds for helping people change, break their fears and insecurities and prepare them for something greater.

Brig points out that the MLM industry is a *"soft entry into your own business."* The success rate is not very high. Within 5 years only 10-15% of those who started are still at it and making some money. The SBA saying that normal Small Businesses have 80% closers with 5 years, so it's not much different.

The MLM lure and appeal of many product companies is money, wealth, success and traveling with friends and like-minded people. Sometimes the leaders make more money on selling training tapes and testimonies to their down line than making money on the product commissions. Brig continues, *"If you were going to make it, you had to learn how to change. For many the inspiration and hype drew out an inner desire to prove themselves. But nearly anyone who put effort into recruiting others has been changed. Failure does lead to success."*

It was their Rocky Soil experience and even when they did not succeed, they learned more about themselves, their capabilities and were inspired with the idea of being their own boss and owning their own business. For most, Rocky Soil is just a failure stage that changes people from the inside out and they recognize how to get ahead through chasing a Dream—God given vision. Perhaps another vision or dream God places in their heart and soul, one day. Or they learn to appreciate their job more and how to overcome some of their weaknesses. The MLM business gives anyone a chance. You don't need $50,000 to start or paid staff, office or big overhead.

Rocky Soil can be the 'Stepping Stones' for something greater God has for you.

Sheep among wolves

Sheep are considered to be meek and meant to follow their Shepherd. It's one of the Lord's examples of being obedient to His leading. In Matthew it says, *"I am sending you out like sheep among wolves. Therefore be as shrewd as serpents (snakes, evil) and as innocent as doves* (loving, Holy Spirit)."

As Sheep in business we are to seek his calling and know his ways—take orders from Him and we will be safe and effective. But there will become times when you must be shrewd to the world's ways of theft, lying, cheating and other tactics that will be used against you. Be wise and smart in your dealings—as the serpent—but still do it with kindness and the love of the Holy Spirit which represents the dove or in this case the sheep.

The Key to Wisdom

OPEN **AREA** You and I meet and learn about each other	**BLIND** **SPOT** You see things about me that I don't recognize
FACADE Things you don't see in me because I hide them	**ONLY GOD KNOWS** None of us knows the future, but God does if we seek Him together

Try the Kitchen table again

Few know the true story of Bill Bowerman and his God-given vision. Bill was well known during the 1970s as the track coach at the University of Oregon. But Bill was constantly frustrated with the injuries to his athletes. It was hard to keep all his athletes on the track at the same time. He attributed many of the problems to the skimpy shoes of his day because they had no real support. His runners suffered constant muscle pulls and ankle problems.

One day, he believed he had received a vision from the Lord that would help remedy the problem. He began designing a new shoe, which was much lighter and more durable. Bill used his waffle iron to indent the lightweight foam material for the base of the shoe. Initially, he became very discouraged because manufacturers said that it cost too much and would never sell. His rocky soil was the voice of criticism and pessimism of hardhearted people.

So, Bill forgot about making the shoes. But one day, as he was trying to encourage his team before a big meet, he quoted a scripture about running the race in such a way as to win the prize. As he drove home that day, he believed that scripture was meant for him and that the Lord was telling him not to give up on the shoes. To go back to his kitchen table and try again to develop those lighter but stronger shoes, more flexible and more supportive. When he took his taped sample to the track his athletes were very encouraging. His miler Phil Knight and Bill never gave up. That's the 'seed vision' of how the Nike shoe company first began. Bill gave God the credit for the vision and the faith to preserve through all types of obstacles.

Truly successful people see problems as stepping-stones not obstacles. In fact, obstacles can lay the foundation for blessings. When a caterpillar becomes a butterfly, it must work hard to emerge from the cocoon. If you break open the cocoon, the butterfly will die. Why? The struggle gives it strength and prepares it to survive in the world. It's the same for us.

Isaiah 40:30-31

"Even youths grow tired and weary,
and young men stumble and fall; but those who
hope in the LORD will renew their strength.
They will soar on wings like eagles; they will run
and not grow weary, they will walk and not be faint."

Learning Teamwork for Success

As a young boy, Pat Kelly's mother dropped him and his brother off at the Virginia Home for Boys, an orphanage because his single mother felt she could not raise them and work after his dad had left them. When Pat was 18 years old, he visited his dad when he was on his deathbed. Most of his life, Pat was resentful for his father and God. For many of us, our image of an earthly father is the image we perceive of our heavenly Father. For Pat, this early life experience was part of his rocky soil.

At the boys' home, he learned to share with other kids, win them over, and be tough and gutsy without parents to shelter or protect him. He had to grow up fast and unspoiled. Pat left the orphanage feeling that he would prove to the world that he was worthy of love and respect. He left with a determined courage and hope. Some might even call it a fear of failure.

In his late 1970s, Bill Riddell, a former employee of Pat, urged him to become a part of a start-up company, Physician Sales and Service. Pat became the CEO because of his experience and guts. He learned very quickly and had enormous faith in their vision for a $500 million international business. John had the privilege of coaching him in his CEO round-table process for eight years. Within 15 years, his company had grown from $2 million in sales to $2 billion.

The rocky soil in his life actually developed his leadership style to help build a dynamic company. His early life experiences formed a determined, positive, focused, and resourceful person. He constantly inspired people and instilled teamwork throughout the company. It was the hard and rocky soil of living in the orphanage, his later experience in the army in Vietnam, and being fired from a corporate job that motivated him more.

Rock Removal

Pat Kelly has an Irish heritage. If you ever visit Ireland, you'll notice that rocks are everywhere in the soil. Though the soil is excellent for potatoes, for years farmers have been removing the rocks to grow their crops. They used them to create rock fences and barriers in order to get them out of the fields. It could be some of the toughness that Pat's ancestors faced that he bears in his spirit.

Instead of giving up on growing crops and potatoes, the Irish farmers simply picked up the rocks and moved them. When obstacles or rocks are in your path, just pick them up and move them aside. What obstacles are you facing? Ask God why they are there and what you should do. Are you letting the rocks keep you from your mission? Can you pick them up and move them aside?

Some people spend their lives actually reprogramming the negative thinking from what they have heard from their mom, dad, or family. Negative messages act like rocks and obstacles that drive them to prove themselves in life. Money too often becomes the measure of their worth and success. We could tell you about a number of entrepreneurs who have made many millions trying to prove their self-worth.

Our self-image can become our god if we let it. We are often ignorant to the truth and principles that our founding fathers are still speaking to us from their graves. There are no self-made millionaires. No man is an island. Life takes a team. This is contrary to the world's perspective that *"it's all about me."* There is a grand design that involves calling, purpose, vision, hope, patience, and persistence. By overcoming obstacles that brings growth and accomplishment, God works in you to accomplish His plans. Whether you know Him or not, He still loves us and is active in our lives.

Can't Admit My Mistakes

John heard a highly respected University professor say that he had a number of conversations with a fellow professor of philosophy about the purpose of our lives in serving Christ. He told this colleague about the peace, love, and joy that he discovered in his relationship with Christ and how it brought real purpose in life.

The philosophy professor finally concluded, *"What you said makes a lot of sense. But If I were to do what you suggest, I would look like a fool and have to admit to my students and friends that I was wrong about so many things. It would be embarrassing. I'd rather not change because I'm comfortable where I am."* The philosophy professor was receiving good seed. However, the rocky soil of his comfortable and prideful heart couldn't nurture it, so it withered.

This is the same thinking for a lot of CEOs who think humility is a sign of weaknesses rather than strength. Most employees admire humility, honesty and a leader willing to act human and open to the ideas and thinking of those on the firing line with the customer.

Come to Jesus

After Howard Schultz purchased Starbucks, the Seattle coffee retailer, from his former employer, he experienced enormous problems.

"I went a year without a salary and could barely make payroll. My wife was the breadwinner that first year. Then my in-laws visited from Ohio. My father-in-law took me aside for my 'come to Jesus' meeting and asked me when was I going to give up on this hobby of mine? However, we stayed the course and raised some more capital. I was embarrassed and humbled at the same time. But we weathered the storm and finally got beyond break-even."

Breaking through the rocky soil does not mean a company has to quit, even though many do. It was a time to find ways to survive, to pray, to seek Wise Counsel, to hustle, scratch and claw until a breakthrough comes. Believe that your purpose is a God Purpose. The Lord uses trials and tribulations to help mature all of us whether you believe in him or not—He can still and will use us.

Psalm 23

"The LORD is my shepherd, I lack nothing.
He makes me lie down in green pastures,
he leads me beside quiet waters, he refreshes my soul.
He guides me along the right paths for
his name's sake..." CONTINUED

Hit in the head with a brick

Steve Jobs was faced with some of the worst rocky soil experiences ever when he was fired in 1985 from Apple, the company he cofounded. But he never stopped innovating. It was in his nature. No one predicated the iPhone, iPad or iPod.

Steve shared some of his best insights as a commencement speaker at Stanford University in 2005, when he said— *"Sometimes life hits you in the head with a brick. Don't lose faith. I'm convinced that the only thing that kept me going was that I loved what I did. You've got to find what you love. Your time is limited; so don't waste it living someone else's life. Don't be trapped by dogma—which is living with the results of other people's thinking. Don't let the noise of others' opinions drown out your own inner voice. And, most important, have the courage to follow your heart and intuition. They somehow already know what you truly want to become. Everything else is secondary."*

Thank God for Unanswered Prayer

Bill Kilgannon, Founder of a successful and fast growing construction company tells of his early experience of his firm start up.

Bill recalls, *"we were well qualified and thought we would obtain three contracts of project right in our sweet spot. We had prayed hard and believed the Lord would bless us with those deals, and we were in shock when we did not get any of the contracts. So we had to revamp our plans and work hard to find other projects.*

Finally, we got on track. But within nine months we got word that each of those three contracts broke down in one form or another. A bank pulled it's financing, EPA stymied another and finally a CEO went to jail over a feud case that caused the company to put a freeze on the last project. It has confirmed our faith in the Lord that he will bless and protect our blind side. No matter how hard it gets, we must trust in the one who created us and brought us this far. In reality the Lord, kept us out of some incredibly Rocky Soil which could have killed our vision."

Rocky Soil Success again and again

David Neeleman was told he had ADD (Attention Deficit Disorder) as a kid in school and most people who have worked for him have agreed. But I believe most Entrepreneurs are ADD or have remnant behaviors of being so. Too many ideas or innovations can drive big companies crazy but not a good entrepreneur team who *"Thrive on Chaos."*

What makes David different than most of us is that he has started or been part of four major airlines all with huge early success. David is Mormon and spent two years in Brazil as a church missionary. He was a college drop out who had early success selling condos and traveled to Hawaii and LA as a part of Morris Airlines, which he and his partners sold to Southwest Airlines. After being fired for too many ideas and visions, he joined a new Canadian start up called West Jet. When his non-compete ended, he raised nearly $120 million to start a New York based airline know as Jet Blue.

Six years later, he was let go over operational issues. Recently, he started Azul Air in Brazil from the same pattern as Jet Blue. It has already had a great impact on Brazil and is boosting their economy.

Every place David Neeleman has gone he has produced change. He literally changed the airline industry in the USA. He claims that he learned you have to have a mission—a cause that drives you forward to serve people and help their lives become better. His life seems to be a series of starts and stops in Rocky Soil. But sometimes God needs people like that—guts, movers and shakers—start up geniuses.

"Trouble is inevitable but misery is optional"
JOEL OSTEEN, PASTOR LAKEWOOD FELLOWSHIP CHURCH

Cleaning Up

In 2006, Donnie Deutsch, who heads his own New York based Advertising and Media business hosted his own TV show on CNBC called the *"The Big Idea."* He interviewed Entrepreneurs and personalities around stimulating ideas for Small Businesses. It was a good show but did not have good enough ratings to continue in its time slot.

But we tell you this to share an amazing story about a young women and her break through idea and marketing determination to get her new product in the right hands. I have tried to find the story and her name and product but been unable to do so. But more important it's about learning from her idea that could change anyone's life.

Let's call her Jeanie, her son had severe headaches and would regularly throw up before going to school in the morning. The doctor thought that it was allergies and unfortunately every drug they tried only made things worse. Her grandmother told her to stop using the popular cleaner she used in the house because it was her problem. She told her to use a natural cleaner like hydrogen peroxide and add apple cider to create a refreshing odor. She and her mother's mother used it for years.

So Jeanie tried it and it did the job. She was so excited she started to share it with neighbors. They were so enthused they asked her to make and sell some to them. Before she knew it, her garage was loaded with inventory and she was getting overwhelmed. Jeanie needed relief. So she called a major manufacturer of cleaning products. They gave her the name of the new products manager but she could never get to talk to him or get an appointment.

Months went by and she could not take it anymore, so she told her husband, I am going to Chicago and meet with this guy. So Jeanie flew to Chicago and stayed at a hotel near the company headquarters. When she arrived unannounced the receptionist was kind but said, *"Unfortunately, Mr. Johnson has appointments all day and won't be able to see you."* Jeanie replied, *"Just tell him I am here and I will wait all day if I have to—to see him for just a few minutes only of his time."*

Jeanie waited nearly the whole day and never got to see him and it made her so mad that she went back the next day and she got the same story from the receptionist. But this time she asked, "What does he look like?" Then she waited by the men's restroom for nearly three hours. Finally, a man who fit the description entered the bathroom and—yes—she followed him inside and confronted him. She told him why she was there. With no other choice, he agreed to give her a 20-minute meeting in his office.

He became so enthused about her cleaning solution, that the company bought the rights to the product. This is a great example of getting through the rocky soil with perseverance.

In James 1:2-3 it says, *"Consider it pure joy, my brothers and sisters,[a] whenever you face trials of many kinds, 'because you know that the testing of your faith produces perseverance. 4 Let perseverance finish its work so that you may be mature and complete, not lacking anything."*

Failing Forward to Seed Faith

As a young boy, Paul Davis grew up convinced he was dumb and ugly. At 16, he joined the merchant marines and served in both the Atlantic and Pacific theatres of World War II. When he came home he learned the lumber business gaining self esteem checking invoices and then estimating. But during the next few years he struggled in the building supply business trying to make a living yet had the unique experience of building 7 houses for some insurance executives moving to town.

Next he tried selling insurance. He said, *"I tried, but just wasn't very good. Then they thought I could be good at training, so they let me do that but not very well. Then a new group asked me to be the General Agent of a new insurance office. But I learned that was not my talent either."*

Finally, sitting in Church one Sunday Paul heard the Pastor share, *"Seek Ye first His kingdom and His righteousness, and all these things will be given to you."* (Matthew 6:33) Paul said, *"As I sat in church that morning, I told the Lord in my heart that's what*

CHAPTER 7 — ROCKY SOIL

I want, your righteousness...It was the turning point in my life and the seed faith I needed to persevere." Soon after, Paul's builder friend Bob was suffering from a lack of work during a downturn. He was frustrated, and asked Paul, who had sales experience, to help him find renovation jobs. Paul recalled, *"Our first job was helping a lady for $165. An Insurance adjuster appreciated our work " and said "I have more work for you."* Their next job was to rebuild a Dentist's office that had fire and water damage.

That was just the beginning of what became Paul Davis Restoration Services. His key customers were insurance companies to restore fire and smoke damaged buildings. Paul sold the business in 1996 with over 100 franchisees and $240 million in revenue, today it reaches nearly a Billion with over 300 franchises world wide.

What Paul did not realize was that God had a plan to use his rocky soil and thorny frustrations experiences of failing forward in construction and insurance. He says, *"I did not realize the Lord was active in my life from day one. He was preparing to create a new industry to help many families and businesses rebuild and help Franchisees find the stable employment I could not find, in my early years."*

Persevering through Failure

Few people know that R. H. Macy, son of a New England Whaler and Quaker started and failed at the retail business at least four times, plus four other types of businesses until he finally moved to New York City in 1858 to try again at the urging of a friend. He was raised in Massachusetts and after failed retail experiences, chased gold in California, Wisconsin, and then back east to begin again in NYC. He left a legacy of the largest retail store in the world—one million square feet—and the largest department store chain of all.

He claimed to have learned tenacity through every experience. His stops and starts represent the ultimate of moving though and learning from rocky soil and beyond. This is an example of the perseverance and never quit attitude necessary to achieve what Jesus was telling all of us is the Secret to the Kingdom in parable of the sower. It's the strength many of us will need to exhibit, if we want to achieve the True Wealth the Lord has in store for us.

> *"If you don't love what you are doing,*
> *you will quit too soon.*
> *If you love what you do,*
> *its not work but a passion you can't let go."*
>
> STEVE JOBS, CO-FOUNDER OF APPLE COMPUTERS

Hindrances to inspiring ideas

The Bible is the number one selling book in America every year and it illustrates the 'false idols' we worship that limit our effectiveness in receiving the Lord's visions for a new business idea or making changes in your life to perserve or allow yourself to improve.

These are called the seven sins of the heart.

1. **Pride** and **Egotism** are the opposite of Humility, openness or teach ability. Some times that comes from fear of looking stupid. Otherwise, its blind overconfidence and thinking you are too smart to undertake what seems like a small idea that won't pay dividends.

2. **Gluttony** and **Addictions** are the result of people feeling lonely, hopeless and needing to feed their body with something that gives them comfort or takes away their pain. Those habits cause them to reject or ignore the visions because of their insecurity or even wanting to quit in the rocky or thorny soil.

3. **Anger** can grip those who heard or were demeaned earlier in their lives. Anger is dangerous where it gets loud around others or causes a person to boil inside. It keeps us from hearing in-

spiring ideas because people are often mad at or looking at those resentfuly.

4. **Lust** is a craving not just for sex but other seducing ideas like money, possessions or success in specific fields. Its an example of what can blind you and cause you to quit too soon or be unwilling to do or pursue some ideas from the Lord or friends or associates.

5. **Laziness** can be caused from mothers or fathers living the same lifestyle. We often pick up the same habits from parents. Or fear can cause someone being afraid to take risk where God wants us to go and contribute to our society.

6. **Envy** is a jealously of what others have and you don't. It can drive some people to accomplish more or be so demeaning that it stymies people from taking risk or over evaluating a vision that they won't pursue because they can't image it make things better.

7. **Greed.** Money is important and useful. The worship of money is against God's plan for us. It causes us to be in a selfish focus and reject many good ideas and concentrate in self-center edways to miss the seed signals the Lord wants to plant in our soul.

These seven sins of our flesh limits our ability to accept new ideas and visions to get through His Secret to the Kingdom of God and the Parable of Sower.

Rocky Soil is Narrow Mindedness
Spiritual direction but not enough faith and persistence

CHAPTER 8

The Thorny Soil

In your journey to become wealthy, you may have encountered both the hard and rocky soil. They are inevitable paths that many people cross. Invariably, you will also experience what Jesus describes as the seed that fell among the thorns. These are relentless weeds that just keep growing. It's another challenging environment for anything to grow and prosper.

THORNY
SOIL

*Entangled thinking
in thorny soil.
Visions grow, but face
many obstacles.*

In the Bible, Jesus says, *"The seed that fell among thorns stands for those who hear, but as they go on their way, they are choked off by life's worries, riches and pleasures, and they do not mature."*

This type of soil may represent physical obstacles of too little capital, poor staff, average products, or no marketing talent. Mental challenges of stubbornness, personal fears, and chasing the false god of money can choke off your seed in the thorny soil. In addition, finding happiness in temporary things or doing it *"my way"* are prime examples of thorns we experience in life.

Some people aren't willing to make the sacrifices to clean out the thorny spots in their lives or businesses. They resist the need to till the soil so things can grow. It was interesting to hear Howard Schultz of Starbucks say, *"Our staff meetings are brutal. We are very self-critical, proactive to change and take on more risk."*

Few people know much about Ted Turner's early life. He was a troublemaker as a teen, in and out of schools. His younger sister died of cancer, which caused him to become, resentful, and angry with God. Ted's father, his hero, committed suicide when Ted was 24 years old. At his father's funeral, Ted realized that he would have to buy out his father's business partners in order to take over the family outdoor advertising business. He had been through the hard soil, rocks, and thorns by the time he was 35 years old. This prepared him for the vision he would eventually receive.

Holding the Vision

In the early 1980s, Ted Turner received an enormous vision and had to break through the thorny soil of criticism that millions of others thought was a very impractical concept. The idea was to start a 24-hour cable news channel around the world (CNN). It took guts and a huge amount of capital to pull it off.

The reason this is so significant is that he brought the world closer together through outlets around the world and made worldwide satellite communications commonplace. Even though he didn't know it, this was God's plan and intention. It proves that God uses what appears to be an arrogant man if He can't find a faithful believer with guts to accomplish His mission.

New Fruit in old Wine Skins

Brig Hart writes...Leaving the direct selling business I had built for 20 years was a devastating experience for Lita and I. Plus we had a number of trials and tests to losing money from what we thought were trusted friends and well intended partnerships. There can really be a purpose in God's plan for our pruning and testing. Thorny soil can test your faith, i.e. did I really get the vision I am to follow ? Why are things not working the way I expect ? When can we overcome these thorns and weeds as we long for peace and joy again?

These were the times we were facing. I started to experience tremendous back pain that I could not seem to over come with therapy and professional help. Then came the big one. I was diagnosed with and was operated on for skin cancer also known as melanoma. It was a shock and I was not prepared to die.

But my natural homeopathic physician told me to eat and drink fresh fruit all day long to take in natural antioxidants. Lots of them, all the time ! It was a hard diet because it tasted lousy since I was a meat and potatoes kind of guy. Finally, I hired someone to research a source for the highest source of nutrients and antioxidants.

We discovered 4 possible companies out West that might have the natural products or recipe I needed to rebuild my immune system to let my body overcome the cancer by itself. The last company we visited gave us a weak first impression but when we talked to the founder and tasted their product, it touched us and seemed like a possible solution. I studied and drank high doses of the product for days. It contained the Acai Berry only grown in the Amazon of Brazil. We even went to the Amazon River to check out its authenticity and his process.

My health began to improve dramatically. So we decided to invest money in this new company called MonaVie and bring our marketing experience, systems and friends to the table. Within less than three years we experienced a billion dollars in sales. Over a million people became involved in those years. I am still so thankful for the trials and thorns God allows us to experience to become wiser and more healthy. I would have never seen such an opportunity to help millions without the Lord using us in the midst of our pain and thorny soil.

> *"When it seems the door has been*
> *shut in your face, it may mean that*
> *a new opportunity is coming.*
> *When the Lord shuts one door,*
> *He opens a window."*
>
> BRIG HART, CO-FOUNDER OF USA ASSOCIATION

Cycles of Success

In business, the Parable of the Sower parallels business leadership and is illustrated in the book, Corporate Lifecycles: How and Why Corporations Grow and Die and What to Do About It, by Ichak Adizes. He explains the typical patterns and cycles that businesses go through. Many articles and personal testimonies support the fact that businesses experience these cycles and seasons of life.

I am not sure whether Ichak Adizes ever read the Parable of the Sower, but his practical teachings align with Jesus' teachings about life and the pursuit of true success. These cycles demonstrate the two-steps-forward-and-one-step-back events in our lives. Even the corporate giants like IBM face these issues and make mistakes.

Blinded by Success

In the 1980s, IBM was one of the top corporations in the world. They were probably the most respected company in America at the time. All of the executives wore dark suits and adopted a policy to never fire anyone. Cornering the market, they were experts at manufacturing, selling, and servicing mainframe computers. They offered the best service for the highest price, and their stock price was always strong.

Ultimately, the thorns of arrogance created from life's riches, pleasures, and deceit choked off their good judgment. They passed on the opportunity to build a software business that instead went to a young Bill Gates. They willingly relinquished all of the PC computer opportunities to Apple, Compaq, HP, and Toshiba along with many others. In error, IBM predicted that the personal computer would never overtake the mainframe computer or be a large share of the business-to-business marketplace.

How could they have failed so miserably? The answer: They were caught up in egotism and riches. The top executives were all making million dollar salaries. After Tom Watson and his son, who built the company, left the company, selfishness and internal politics killed their entrepreneurial spirit along with their openness to visions and innovations. As a result, the business began its decline. Within a 12-year period, they went from 420,000 employees to 200,000 employees. Eventually they learned from the difficulties they endured in the thorny soil. Today, they've re-grown with a new entrepreneurial spirit and merged into different niches in the business market.

If the seeds of our visions can't build strong roots in the rocky soils or withstand the choking effect of the thorns, our thinking is distorted and the shadows of gloom are brought in to view. The bureaucratic stage of a corporation's life cycle binds it in the chains of policies and procedures, which bring forth egotism and prevent healthy change. The Lord wants to move the world forward. If the soil of our heart is beaten down, we will reject innovations and creativity for new growth. When growth declines, companies try to survive by reorganizing and downsizing to achieve profit projections.

The more that companies are blinded by success and publicity, the greater the presence of corporate politics, resentment, jealousy, and bitterness. Those are some of the thorny internal issues that create cancers that can take good companies down. Public companies have such great pressure to fudge the numbers and to justify their decisions. They can't see the forest (thorns, weeds, and tall grass) through the trees.

> **"Success is a lousy teacher.**
> **It seduces smart people**
> **into thinking they can't lose."**
> —BILL GATES

Knocked Out For Success

Can you imagine playing college football at Colorado University against Oklahoma and getting knocked out on the field? For a short time, you lie there as the trainers and medical people try to revive you. But you are deep in thought as God speaks to you and tells you that you are going to be a great businessman one day. Finally, you come to and are ushered off the field. Would God take such a moment to speak and give you a vision?

That's just the way it happened to Al Hollingsworth, who had a relationship with the Lord. That experience was a turning point in his life and one that he never has forgotten. Al's grandfather was a sharecropper in Mississippi, and his parents lived on the rough side of the tracks in Omaha. That knockout experience caused him to get serious about academics, and he proudly graduated with a business degree.

Due to his belief in God's plan for his life, he even turned down an offer to play professional football with the New York Giants in order to pursue business. For a good-looking young Afro-American in the sixties he chose the road that wasn't considered cool. But, within a few short years, he started his own packaging business. He relocated to California and hired a beautiful assistant, Hatti, to whom he later proposed. The rapid success of his business drew the attention of the media and other businessmen, as well as the governor's office. He was sought after by various business boards, he spoke often about how to become a successful entrepreneur.

Though he didn't know it, he was acquiring all the thorns and weeds of notoriety, money, and possessions of the super rich. Al lost touch with the Lord because he was too busy chasing the world's model for wealth. He could not see it, but his egotism and invincible thinking was producing a real briar patch of thorns and its *"knockout hit"* called bankruptcy. Often the biggest problems that successful people have in hearing God is learning to quiet the noise inside their heads—the drive for success, power, and affluence.

Through the loss of his business, his heart was broken as he spent the next year talking and praying, *"Oh, Lord, what have I done? Where did I get off the path of your calling?"* He prayed on mountaintops, in the desert, in his car, and in church. He devoured his Bible for answers and direction while asking for forgiveness.

Finally, the Lord told him to return to the packaging business and start over. He realized that this time his business was called to be different. This time he was to pursue the Lord's leading and use his leadership ability, charisma, and charm for ministering opportunities. This time he was to be faithful and wise rather than successful and self-absorbed.

The Lord told him something very profound, which he believes exemplifies God's ultimate purpose for everyone. He said to Al, *"You take care of my business* (God's ministry opportunities), *and I will take care of your business"* (man's opportunity to make a living, grow in business, and achieve the world's economic standards for success).

Today, Al's business, Aldelano Packaging Corporation, is successful by the world's view with six plants across the country and has many as 1,500 people on the payroll. There are no cash flow issues because Al is his own banker. But most important to Al and Hatti is their ministry, BOSS the Movement (BOSS stands for Building On Spiritual Substance.) The mission is to teach young people about the inner motivation to be successful by God's standards while achieving and living in the world. They travel the world teaching trainers to carry the message forward, especially in Southeast Asia and the United States. This time, they are on the covers of magazines to open the door for His greatest purposes.

Ephesians 1:18

"I pray that the eyes of your heart may be enlightened
in order that you may know the hope
to which he has called you,
the riches of his glorious inheritance
in his holy people."

Economic Blunder or Genius among the Thorns ?

Between 1908 and 1916, Henry Ford moved to transform the automobile industry through his new automation process and by reducing the cost of Model T cars by 58%. He drew criticism from the financial experts and in the face of shareholder suits against his practice while doubling the wage of the average worker. He wanted autos to be affordable to the average consumer.

The **Wall Street Journal** accused Henry Ford of *"economic blunders if not crimes"* which would soon *"return to plague him and the industry he represents as well as organized society."* Ford they continued. had injected *"spiritual principles into a field where they do not belong—a heinous crime."* Ford may have been one of the key executives to help build a middle class society in America.

He successfully, went against those on Wall Street focused on greed which was the major contributor to the Great Depression 13 years later. Amazingly, the same false god of greed took down our US economy twice, during the stock market crash of 1929 which lead to the depression and later in 2008 when Fannie Mae and Banks created the *"Great Mortgage Crisis."* (reference Built to Last).

The Deceit Factors

Between 1995 and 2001, a national association approached John three times, asking him to help them develop nationwide CEO roundtable groups. The first couple of times, he had to say that I did not feel called. Besides, he also had a non-compete agreement that would preclude him from that pursuit. By the third time, years later, he knew he had been called to build and develop Wise Counsel, and his non-compete was no longer in force.

So, he prayed and felt this was part of his calling. Within six months, he had successfully navigated through the rocky soil, but didn't realize he was about to be in the midst of thorns. His company had borrowed money for expansion to set up the infrastructure he needed. But something blind sided him.

Traces of jealousy, greed, and deceit were beginning to affect the thinking of the new strategic partner from the top down. He heard pieces of conversations, but it was never discussed with him firsthand. We had quickly acquired clients in Colorado and North Carolina, but no matter how smart he was or how hard he tried, he could not seem to develop leaders to launch in the mid- and pacific west.

After 18 months, he knew in his spirit that the strategic partnership was ending. The question was why and how to step away in a win-win conclusion. Rather than meeting it head on, he procrastinated and sought to find the diamond in the rough. Then, in the only negative conversation in two years, the partnership ended. Those experiences leave indelible warning signs, such as, *"Don't do that again!"* Partnerships often seem to fail, but there is often something to learn that hopefully makes us better and more effective in the future. The Bible says don't be unequally yoked. Even though we appeared to have the compatible missions to be equally yoked, the thorns can choke off true success.

Third World Busistry

Curt Coleman had a very successful Hair Salon business with over a hundred employees and 8 stores. Some of his key clients were celebrities but when one of his people died of AIDS, the word spread like wildfire among his clients. The business declined rapidly. He was caught in a very difficult situation as he closed all but one store.

Facing possible bankruptcy with mountains of debt. he did not know where to turn. But a High School friend heard about his troubles and called to say he wanted to visit Curt and tell him about Jesus. Curt said to himself *"Oh no, not Jesus."*

But his troubles got worse, so he finally let his friend visit. Curt was very touched and made the commitment to Christ. Within weeks he attended a Prayer breakfast where a missionary talked about his work in Peru. He asked for volunteers who would come with him on his next trip for 30 days. Curt was moved and told the missionary he would love to go but had no money. Another friend over heard them and gave Curt the money to go with the missionary.

The experience changed him and on his final day in Peru, he saw some Americans trying to take advantage of a poor lady selling her bracelets. In disgust, Curt intervened and asked the lady how much she wanted for all her bracelets. It took his last $50.

He had no choice but to sell the bracelets at his remaining Hair Salon. Curt was shocked that the bracelets sold out in just a few days at which his wife said, *"You may have a business here."* Then a local retailer said, *"I will buy hundreds of items if you get them for me from Peru."*

So with no money, he headed back to Peru and asked the village people to make the items he needed and allow him 30 days to pay. They finally agreed and when he returned, he shockingly discovered the buyer had gone bankrupt. In desperation he tried to sell the merchandise to other retailers. No one was buying.

Devastated he headed home but felt the Lord pulling on his heart to stop at a last strip shopping center. There he met a landlord willing to offer him a small store front for a month to month lease. He felt the Lord was opening the door. Within a month he sold enough merchandise to pay his suppliers in Peru.

Thus was the birth of *"Go Fish"* which is now an international franchise business with 20 stores buying from 7 countries. Curt witnesses, prays and serves his suppliers by paying their requested price. Curt is bringing the world together in God's plan using his faith to survive the thorny and rewarding life he's been called to.

Business + Ministry = Busistry

Recessions, the predictable chaos

Recessions come on an average of every 8-10 years. It may be the one predictable negative to a Free Enterprise System. The government can't stop it so it will affect entrepreneurs, employees and the spending power of a whole society. It's normally caused from businesses being too aggressive, growing too fast or racing to capture more 'market share.' Successful leaders can drift into the false god of greed. The economy gets overheated like a car racing at 140 mph when it's only built for 120 mph.

The solution—it's time to go on a diet and stop the 'overindulging' and slim down. You might say that Joseph, (the Biblical story and son of Abraham) handled the first recession based on interpreting Pharaoh's dream. But God had given Joseph the gift of interpretation. From the dream he recognized there was going to be a great famine where thousands of people would lose their lives. So he planned for the seven years event by setting aside 10% of the harvest each year creating a supply to allow the nation to get through the drought with much less suffering, while other nations faced chaos.

Recessions are rocky soil for most businesses and thorny soil for others, depending on the industry and weaknesses in the economy. Some industries continue to escape the trend like health care has done during this most recent recession. The downturns are another character development experience the Lord warned us of, but confirms we would learn more perseverance—which will help shape the future of our lives—for bigger and better things to come.

The greatest wireless tool ever conceived.

David Green, the founder and CEO of Hobby Lobby, the $2.5 Billion retailer operating in nearly 30 states tells in his book More than a Hobby and how he grew his family business as a start up in Oklahoma City in 1972. Out of the gate they found a niche in picture frames that grew into retail locations.

The economy in the oil producing states in the early 80's was very good. No matter what they did, Hobby Lobby consistently grew and made money. But in the mid 80's things changed as oil prices went down and the economy was hurting in many parts of the country. With several locations and $25 million in gross sales they lost money for the first time. They could not pay their suppliers all that they owed.

David said, *"It seemed like nothing I tried would work. My nerves were shot. Every time the phone rang, I knew it was another creditor wanting payment. I was toast. Some nights I doubt if I slept a total of one hour. The only thing I knew to do was to pray, 'God what do you want me to learn from this?' I would leave the office and walk alone in Eldon Lyon Park, crying out for help and guidance. Other times, I would literally crawl under my desk to plead with God. It was a way of getting alone for prayer without people watching me."*

His wife and family reminded and comforted David many times of something he had already said for years... *"It's God's business and it's His choice how it will succeed or fail."* His job was to be a good steward and be obedient to Him. We may think we are in control, but in the final analysis we are not. Thorny soil will be a part of any ones' life but it depends on how we deal with it that counts.

Ridiculous Success

Fred Smith, the founder of Federal Express, claims he received the vision for the company while a student at Yale University. It came from a class assignment when he wrote a proposal for a new business. His rocky soil preparation experience came next in the Marines and Vietnam. The Marines taught him mental toughness, to never quit, and to lead in times of adversity in the thorny soils of life.

He said, *"In retrospect, it was ridiculous to try and put this system together that required so much money and changes in government regulations. But at the time, I did not know that. I was a zealot."* This story is often shared. One time, when he could not make payroll, he flew to Las Vegas in desperation and came back with enough winnings to make it through until the next pay period. He just had to accomplish a great feat. Today, he has 170,000 employees and $160 billion in sales. Fred demonstrates that the power of a vision and faith made sure his system would work.

Pulling Weeds

The Bible says that both seed and weed grow together in the beginning. When harvest time arrives, we are to pull and burn the weeds first, and then gather the wheat. Likewise, in business, we should establish our customer base, the quality of our products, and our reputation before making serious changes. Get through the rocky soil first and allow the roots to penetrate deeply. Growth is critical in a business start up, but disturbing the soil too much in the beginning could damage the roots of the wheat.

We all dislike thorny soil and pulling weeds. It's not fun. Even though it is rewarding afterward, the weeds just keep coming back. Where are you among the thorns in your business? Weeds can represent deceit, bitterness, arrogance, (internal or external), poor cash flow, lousy marketing, or lack of good communication. Some thorns are characterized by the inability to change.

At this stage of growth, you may need to spend more time searching for and hiring outstanding and talented people for game-breaker positions that can make or break your company. Sometimes it involves knowing your pricing. Years ago, a top consultant said that too many owners price their products based on their cost rather than the perceived value to the customer. Another problem area for many business owners is being unfocused. We've made this mistake many times by devoting our time and energy to nonessentials, rather than my top three priorities.

Pruning for New growth

If you have ever watched a farmer trim his trees you understand why he would cut the dead branches. But why would he also cut the branches producing the best fruit? In John 15, he explains, *"I am the true vine, and my Father is the gardener. 2 He cuts off every branch in me that bears no fruit, while every branch that does bear fruit he prunes[a] so that it will be even more fruitful. 3 You are already clean because of the word I have spoken to you. 4 Remain in me, as I also remain in you. No branch can bear fruit by itself; it must remain in the vine. Neither can you bear fruit unless you remain in me."*

If you're in business and you have lost customers, had your supply chain disrupted or boycotted because of your stand on marriage, you probably feel you are being pruned. In many cases the answers are yes. God could be setting you up for greater growth that will bare new fruits and more customers and clients

Don't Be Choked

Sometimes the rocky soil and thorns that choke off the success of your vision are not there because the Lord is trying to test you, but because of other factors. Your poor attitude and the lack of cooperation of your partners can cause rocks and thorns to choke your business dream. Fear from the enemy, or 'rocks and thorns,' breed skepticism in the life of your organization steering it away from developing to it's fullest. God's vision is farsighted, but we are nearsighted.

I love the beautiful green ivy in the front of our home, but every spring the thorns and weeds try to take it over. Too many of us think that since we've planted with good intentions, our marriages, our families, or our businesses will stand the test of time. That is a false sense of security. We need to make changes and improvements by uprooting the constantly growing weeds or thorns. We must overcome adversity by replanting, re-tilling the soil, and even using a weed killer.

Overcoming Obstacles

If you look at some of the best-run businesses, families, churches, and ministries they are always in a state of self-examination. Not just their numbers, but also their mission. They welcome the opinion of their employees and customers. These businesses and organizations boldly ask the questions, *"How can we get better? What changes do we need to make?"*

Do you notice that if you keep tilling the soil of your heart (through learning, risk and wise counsel), the thorns and weeds can't take root? We find that too many people wait on God to make a path in the midst of the weeds. Instead, He is waiting for us to take initiative and clear the weeds so we can see His path

In Genesis, after Adam and Eve rebelled against God, He threw them out of the garden and into the world. God spoke to Adam and said, *"Cursed is the ground because of you; through painful toil you eat of it all the days of your life. It will produce thorns* (that's our word) *and thistles for you and you will eat the plants of the field."* This was written many years before Jesus taught on the Parable of the Sower. To me, it confirms what the Lord is trying to tell us about our pursuit to be a millionaire—that we will experience trials and thorns in our quest. The Bible also says, *"Very little good happens without pain from a bad experience. Yet, good overcomes evil and light over comes darkness. The Lord is full of compassion and mercy."*

1 John 1:5
"God is light; in him there is no darkness at all."

John 8:12
"I am the light of the world. Whoever follows me will never walk in darkness, but will have the light of life."

The Threshing Floor

The Bible has numerous references to the threshing floor as they laid the wheat and other harvest on the flat and hard floor and beat with sticks or even oxen walking on the kernels to crack open the husks so the seed or edible grain could be gathered. They even waved the grains in the air to separate the wheat from the husk. There was no machinery in Bible times to separate the wheat from the chaff.

It may seem to many of us that the rocky and thorny soil are just like we are put upon the threshing floor to get to the meat of what God wants and places with in us. Is the parallel here from Jesus saying that pursuing the purpose of the seed the Lord has given you—representing the visions and unctions of the Lord to take and execute His plan—going to be like being beaten on our own threshing floor, i.e. hard work, beaten down sometimes, a rough and painful experience? If not physically but mentally and spiritually?

Engineer to Entrepreneur

For more than 10 years, John had the privilege of working with Mark Mullins. Mark was a native of the Midwest who relocated from Cummings Engineering group to Florida through the purchase of a trailer manufacturing company. As a professional manager with great operational experience, he had the dream and vision to be an entrepreneur. But he went through eight years of struggle to make his small manufacturing company successful through the ups and downs of finding good people, creating the systems, marketing, and building good cash flow.

Finally, one day, in his CEO roundtable group, another member urged him to sell that business and take over as the president of his franchising company. It was a hard decision, which meant that he would lose all the money that he had invested. But he plunged forward and helped Paul Davis Systems grow by adding over 100 franchisees. Ultimately, it became one of the best franchise companies in the country. When that company was sold, he had the opportunity to buy one of the small spinoff divisions. Over the next 16 years, he systematically built a highly profitable and sought-after organization. Also, during that time, he became involved in some top ministry and service organizations, like the Salvation Army, Red Cross, and many others. As he gave, his company flourished.

Mark looks back and says, *"If it weren't for that incredible struggle with my small manufacturing firm, I wouldn't be where I am today, pursuing the Lord's greater plans for me."*

Jesus selected 12 men in the marketplace who had no religious education or training. He taught them to be open to God's leading, to develop passion, and to change the lives of others. It's through our zeal for God that we are equipped to remove the thorns from our path. Whether the thorns are inside or outside of us, uprooting them is the only way to attain and maintain success.

Avoiding thorns before they become problems

Pam Mullarkey's life was changed when she was jogging one morning in her neighborhood. A teenager stopped her and urged Pam to go tell the parents across the street that their high school daughter was pregnant and going to get an abortion. Shocked Pam said that's not possible because the girl does not even date anyone. To her surprise and the young girl's parents, the story was true.

That week the Lord woke Pam in the middle of the night to give her a vision for what became Project SOS (Save our Students). For over 15 years, she and her staff have reached over 200,000 students in Northeast Florida and reduced teen pregnancy by 64%. Project SOS staff teach teens how to deal with or avoid sex, drugs and alcohol. They use skits, classroom education and counseling. Pam's program is a model for the nation—and now other nations—for teaching abstinence to young girls and 'refusal skills' before marriage to remain pure.

Get your Soul and thinking open to receive

Check this from Philippians 4:6-9 and decide where your mind or soul is in relationship to the Lord's words... *"Do not be anxious about anything, but in every situation, by prayer and petition, with thanksgiving, present your requests to God. And the peace of God, which transcends all understanding, will guard your hearts and your minds in Christ Jesus.*

Finally, brothers and sisters,

> *whatever is true,*

> *whatever is noble,*

> *whatever is right,*

> *whatever is pure,*

> *whatever is lovely,*

> *whatever is admirable*

—if anything is excellent or praiseworthy—think about such things.

Whatever you have learned or received or heard from me, or seen in me—put it into practice. And the God of peace will be with you."

Thorny Soil is Double Mindedness
Worldly success ignites the battle between good and evil

CHAPTER 9

Finally!
The Good Soil

The last part of Jesus' Parable of the Sower reveals what happens when our seed falls on good soil. This happens when the seed—God's voice, vision, instructions, or intention—is planted in the good soil of our heart.

"But the seed falling on good soil refers to someone who hears the word and understands it. This is the one who produces a crop, yielding a hundred, sixty or thirty times what was sown."

Humble and teachable thinking.
Visions led by the Potter's hand to form the nourishing soil of your soul.

GOOD SOIL

Good soil is ready to receive our seed when we see the vision and understand God's truth and purpose. In other words, it happens when our hearts are fully open to the Lord's leading, and we have been willing to pay the price to get to this place. When we are in the good soil, we've developed the mental and spiritual toughness to persistently search for deeper intent. People like Al Hollingsworth reached the good soil. The next challenge is staying there. What helps the seed to grow is not just good soil with its nutrients but the proper balance of sun and rain.

For soil to accept the seed, it must be fertilized, rich in minerals, have proper rain and sun, and be tilled. Soils can be depleted of nutrients after too many years of harvesting the same crop. In fact, there is biblical reference about resting the soil. After every seven years, the soil should remain unused to allow it to replenish itself before a new crop is planted. Some farmers rotate crops with soybeans, for example, to attempt to replace the lost nitrogen and other nutrients.

So, in a good and healthy millionaire business, what represents the sun, rain, tilling, nutrients, and crop rotation? They could be things like: attitude, inspiration, praise, goal settings, incentives, bonuses, surveys, good results, recognition, and new product development. Doesn't this sound like a healthy organization that is helping and growing customers and people while overcoming obstacles?

We believe in order to get to the fourth level, the 'good soil,' God tests and challenges us. He allows us to face significant obstacles to make us stronger and fertile. The seed He plants in our heart grows into an idea or vision that becomes a reality on the earth. If we allow ourselves to remain in beaten down soil, we will never see success. If we have journeyed enough to the point of reaching the good soil, we should be prepared to realize the next vision. In the good soil, we do not allow the thorns, rocks, and obstacles to overcome us.

His grace is sufficient to carry us forward. Although we face more issues, problems, and tough circumstances, we will be ready to become the beautiful butterfly He expected us to be.

Is Good Soil Like Reaching Heaven?

Some of us may want to say that reaching Good Soil is like heaven in business or your career. After getting through the rocks and thorns, everything else is smooth sailing. Millions in growth seem to come easy. Chick-Fil-A has had tremendous growth over the last forty-five years going from its first chicken sandwich mall location in 1967 to free standing buildings in 1986. Yet, store sales volume levels for their six days a week of operation have consistently exceeded the national fast food average store volumes for seven days. It pays to not work on Sunday.

Since 2003, when they reached one billion in sales, their growth has been off the charts reaching three billion in sales by 2009, an average of nearly 25% per year. It pays to honor the Lord.

In the early 80's they faced a watershed or rocky or thorny experience when the national competitors started to sell the chicken sandwich, which they had first created. Sales were flat for the first time in history. Their Board met in a strategic planning session and prayed for God's guidance. The result was a mission statement and how they would honor God and that they would eventually create free standing locations. I believe this was the turning point to move them from thorny soil to good soil.

More recently, in a radio interview, Dan highlighted the need for traditional family two parent homes to avoid the *"fatherless"* problem in our nation. Gay rights groups twisted his comments and turned it into a media hype that caused some Mayors to say they did not want Chick-fil-A as a business in their city. They later backed down when they learned the truth. Dan's remarks were being labeled as *"intolerant of gays,"* while he never mentioned gays or alluded to anything negative toward them.

In response to the injustice, Mike Huckabee, former Governor of Arkansas used his media influence to urge supporters to go to Chick-fil-A for an *"Appreciation Day."* Conservative believers came by the millions to support the values of Chick-fil-A. Estimates are that it has spiked sales even higher into the 50% growth range in one day.

> ### *"God often takes negatives and turns them into positives"*
> BRIG HART, CO-FOUNDER OF USA ASSOCIATION

The Valleys are Rich

John's reminded of the story told by Dave Dravecky, the former baseball pitcher for the San Francisco Giants, who lost his pitching arm. After his second comeback attempt following a final bout with cancer, the doctors had to amputate his arm.

Amazingly, he said, *"Cancer has been a blessing. God has given me an opportunity to share His love with so many different people because of my circumstances. You know, a valley for a farmer is a very rich place to plant a crop. When we go through the valleys of life, it is very rich for each of us. Unfortunately, my pride got in my way. I just wanted to be in control. But through my suffering, I have become more like Him. He shapes and molds us in the way He wants us to be. Suffering produces perseverance . . . perseverance produces character . . . and character produces hope. 'Hope will not disappoint us with Him.' We are in process. He is the healer. Through these experiences, I have learned to look at life through an eternal perspective."*

Notice Dave's reference to the soil. When John and his wife were first married, they spent two years in the Peace Corps in Brazil. Near Brasilia, the capital, at about 3,000 feet above sea level. The soil there was hard red clay. It was difficult for the trees to grow. Every summer afternoon the rains came. The valleys were rich, green, and lush because the nutrients washed down into the valleys where the farmers planted and harvested their best crops.

Could the valleys—pains, frustrations, and obstacles—in your life really be God's promised land for you? If we don't go through the valleys, can we really recognize good soil? The disciple Paul, who wrote much of the New Testament, was trapped in deep valleys many times. But it's in that time that we cry out the most. Prison was Paul's most productive time, writing several chapters of the Bible, alone without distraction. Those are the best times for the Lord to work on our hearts.

Holding Back Pain

In 1993, John began his day as usual, doing 20 pushups and stretching exercises. But as he reached down and touch his toes, the pain in his back was so intense that he could not continue. And the pain didn't go away. For seven years, he endured it. He tried everything— chiropractors, acupuncture, x-rays with doctors, and massages. Nothing would take it away. In fact, he couldn't even sit without pain. This happened in the midst of trying times and the eventual sale of his business.

One day, he sensed the Lord's leading to attend a different church. Every Sunday at the new church, the pastor would ask, *"Who needs prayer for healing?"* He'd stand up, but never felt any real change.

Over time, the pain disappeared. A couple of years later his sister, Judy, told him about a book entitled, *Healing Back Pain.* She shared that with her husband, Bill, who had been experiencing deep back pain. He read this book and his pain vanished. Knowing other people with the same issue, John ordered the book. Author Dr. John E. Sarno, has researched back pain for years in Upstate New York and discovered that stress is the main cause of back pain. The American Medical Association has said for years that stress causes 80% of illnesses in America. Stress can impact, headaches, heart disease, ulcers and back pain to name a few. It reduces the flow of the blood supply to different parts of the body. Check You Tube for an interview with Stossel.

When he looks back on those seven years of pain, he realizes that he had been completely pulled out of his comfort zone and very insecure. God had been calling him to write a book and start a brand new business that he had never done before. When he finally yielded to Him and stopped resisting it, the pain just went away and up until then he didn't know why.

Adversity leads to good soil

John Mackey, the founder of Whole Foods, the billion dollar organic—300 store plus—food chain, said he discovered the problem with his first store when he had to close it. *"It was just too small. We needed more selection for the customer."* Never one to give up, he was able to acquire more investors and opened a bigger store. As it started to become successful, along came a rare flood in downtown Austin that wiped out the store. He had no insurance, but by the grace of God and with the help of the SBA and more investors, he reopened the store four months later. Because he was determined to grow that store, nothing deterred him from his mission, not even a flood.

Mackey continues, *"Every type of adversity is an opportunity for you to learn and grow and even get better. Or you contract in your fear and paralyze yourself. You have to have inner faith and determination that you are going to overcome this."*

The seed voices and thoughts of God are speaking to us. They are training us through the up-and-down valleys of life, teaching us how to find or produce the most fertile soil in our hearts and souls. He wants to impregnate us with His purpose and plan.

The good soil is not the Promised Land or the Garden of Eden. Instead, it resides in your openness and receptivity. It's about overcoming your fears and self-centered thinking. It's about fruitfulness. In the book of Matthew, the Bible says how you can tell a true believer. *"By their fruit you will recognize them."* It also states, (Gal. 5) *"The fruit of the spirit is love, joy, peace, patience, kindness, goodness, faithfulness, gentleness, and self control."* It goes on to say, *"Since we live by the Spirit, let us keep in step with the Spirit. Let us not become conceited, provoking, and envying each other."*

The Long Preparation for Harvest

Henry P. Crowell had seven years of preparation to reach good soil. In the early 1900s, his father died of tuberculosis. The doctors warned Henry that there was a very good chance that he would get the same disease in his early twenties. The best cure would be for him to leave Cleveland, go west, and live outdoors for seven years. It was tough for Henry, who had to pass up the opportunity to attend Yale University, but he knew the biblical significance of seven years.

Through the valleys of Henry's life, his passion became a deep-hearted desire to serve the Lord. He considered the journey to be his divine appointment. Friends prayed for him as he sought to breathe normally during those years of frustration away from his family. He took odd jobs on ranches and farms. He gained experience in business by buying and selling two farms in North Dakota. Henry prayed often and pledged that if the Lord would allow him to have a business enterprise, he would not name the business after himself.

When he finally returned home, Henry prayed for the right business of his own. Within 30 days, he was offered the opportunity to buy an old run down mill near Akron, Ohio. Adversity had prepared and chiseled his character through the hard, rocky, and thorny soils of life. He felt the confirmation of the Lord in buying the mill. Little did he know that the mill would become a giant known as the Quaker Oats Company.

"One who gains strength by overcoming obstacles possesses the only strength which can overcome adversity."

— ALBERT SCHWEITZER

Can a Lawyer build an Airline?

Herb Kelleher's experience is an in-depth trial of perseverance through the rocky and thorny soils. In only five years, he created one of the most dynamic businesses in the 21st century. Herb was a lawyer by training who, for many years, had a secret passion to have his own business. It was as if he was waiting for the right opportunity.

The soil of his heart was ready because he did not skip the hard and beaten down soil. Instead, he knew that it would prepare him for something better. During his early years while completing law school, he gained some experience with the courts, including the U.S. Supreme Court. This prepared him for the entrepreneurial vision he would receive. After law school, he moved to Texas to open his law practice.

One night while at dinner in San Antonio, his client, Rollin King, suggested that they start an airline. The vision was planted as they sat in the airport. Neither had any experience in the industry. But for some reason, this lawyer received a vision to start an intrastate airline. They found a loophole in the law that convinced them that they could start an airline quickly. After all, it would be a commuter airline within the state. Since they weren't businessmen, they were naive enough to try it. However, they couldn't predict the rocky and thorny soil that Braniff, Continental, and Trans Texas would take them through.

These big airlines filed various lawsuits to stop them. After three and a half years in and out of the courts, they had no money left. Herb's board was ready to throw in the towel. But because of Herb's willingness to take on financial risk personally, they hung on to what many call his absolute tenacity and warrior spirit. The final chapter of this amazing business saga was written at the U.S. Supreme Court.

Herb's company, Southwest Airlines, has changed the airline industry. Based on domestic passengers, it is the largest low-cost airline in the United States. Also, it is the only airline in history that has experienced profitability in its existence. As you study the track record and culture of Southwest Airlines, you have to be amazed at their strategies.

On the New York Stock Exchange, Southwest's ticker symbol is LUV. (Love field is still their hub in Dallas but the word fits perfectly into a God plan). When reviewing their principles, you'll notice that they are nearly word for word in tune with the Bible's definition of love. The company hires people that try to love customers and one another. They broke the mold of most companies, because they seek to love and serve their employees even before their customers.

So many big companies want to downsize their employment to increase their profitability. Oftentimes, they do this to impress their stockholders and receive good publicity. Amazingly, here's an attorney who focused on his people and loyalty to them. Did Herb's tenacity and innovation come from his pursuit of being a millionaire? No. It was the result of surviving through the rocky and thorny soils and persevering through the obstacles of his calling.

Wise Counsel

If you have ever watched the TV show Shark Tank you see how investors are presented opportunities to partner with new business ventures or inventions. Again separating the 'wheat from the chaff.' The wheat was called the meat or edible portion of the harvest and the chaff, the hard outer husk that is less desirable to eat. Jesus in the parable of the wheat and tares (Matt 13:36-43) explains to the manager who explains to the servants not to try and pull up the weeds among the wheat. Instead let them be harvested together and after they will be separated. It seems to me that is the function of Wise Counsel. The Lord led John to create Wise Counsel years ago to help entrepreneurs make better and Biblical based decisions. Fellow entrepreneurs present their plans or ideas to non-competitors in our Wise Counsel and roundtable process. It's easier to see through the eyes of peers who have the heart to see a fellow believer succeed. They want the best for one another. Honest advice and prayer. We ask the Lord to guide us.

The goal is again to be obedient to God's plan and calling. To love the customers, employees, vendors, suppliers and everyone the business or ministry interacts with. Separating the wheat—good ideas or plans—from the chaff—bad, weak or selfish ideas. We can ask, is this a good idea or a God idea? It's lonely as the head of a business and you need outside input to be wise in your decision-making. It's not about just making money but being effective and successful *"in the world, but not of the world...but of His purposes."*

Unexpected Heroes

Most business entrepreneurs would not have tried to start an airline because of the hard soil in their heart and soul. But God needed someone with legal experience and guts to accomplish His mission. We can also see why John Mackey, who was a philosophy major, said, "I am glad I didn't take business in school, it might have limited my thinking and preparation to build Whole Foods."

God knew both John's and Herb's nature. He knew that the bigger their obstacles, the tougher and more determined they'd become. When Herb was asked, *"What is your success in motivating your people?"*

He said, *"A clear set of values, almost a religious creed that we sold, suggested, sang, and shared every day."*

When asked how he made it through the toughest times in building Federal Express, founder Fred Smith said, *"Probably conviction. I was convinced that what I was trying to do with my teammates was important and that it would be successful. The opposite side of that coin is persistence. Very rarely have I ever seen any business or major undertaking that goes in a straight line. There are zigs and zags, victories and defeat, and you have to be propelled by that conviction that what you're doing is right and what you're doing is important, and to persevere in it. That's probably more important than anything else."*

Interestingly, visions and convictions come from the Spirit of the Lord. They grip your heart unless, by your selfish or negative thinking, you reject His movement on your heart and soul. Are you willing to achieve your greatest purpose in life and constantly look for His signals?

Finding the Formula

Putting all of this into perspective: God is a Spirit of love, truth, and life. If your spirit is not committed or open to His Spirit, you will not know for certain when He is communicating with you. It will only seem like a good idea or thought that you can accept or reject. Long before radio, television, cell phones, wireless computers, or satellites, the Lord has been using the airways by His Spirit. He urges us to communicate with Him by prayer, simply talking to Him inwardly and outwardly. His Holy Spirit and angels don't sleep; they are working 24/7.

Here's where the static comes in. We hear three voices about what to do.

1. **First, we listen to our own thoughts or ideas about what we want.** It's the same free will we are born with. The thoughts revolve around the things we want and desire.

2. **The next voice is from the enemy—satan.** If you don't believe in Satan, that's exactly what he wants. His desire is for you to sink into absolute depression, despair to contemplate suicide. On the flip side, he is also very effective at getting you to think evil

of others. But if he can't derail you on your journey to success, he wants you neutralized by binding your free will with worldly passions. Doing so prevents you from seeking God's purpose and divine plan.

3. **The final voice is the voice of the Lord who shares divine thoughts and visions with us.** When you are in covenant with Him, you know when He is speaking to you. Remarkably, even when you don't know Him, He still communicates His will when He has a special destiny for you. It's not always about building a wealthy business, but it may be as simple as helping a neighbor or loving a spouse. He works full time and never gives up on us.

God is determined to get your attention. He can allow you to get knocked out, just like Al Hollingsworth. At the same time, He can speak to you through cancer, an auto accident, nightmare, fire, sickness, or business issue like He did with author Ken Blanchard. He spoke to me about my wife before I ever knew or believed in Him. If He can speak to men like Kent Humphreys and Paul Cuny about selling or discontinuing their businesses—He can speak to leaders of nations, He can whisper to you about little things and insurmountable problems.

Reality Sets In

In 1966, John and Judy Beehner came home from a two year assignment in the Peace Corps in Brazil. Within a week of their return, John came down with severe stomach pain. He spent nearly a week in bed, and the doctor had no answers. His mother- in-law kept insisting that Sprite would settle his stomach. But it made it worse.

The pain was so intense at times he thought he could die. Even though he prayed off and on, he had no relationship or commitment to serving the Lord at that time. Finally, on the sixth day, as he laid in bed, a deep thought came over him. *"You will not die. God is not finished with you yet."* That thought sank deep into his soul and the fear that was gripping him was gone. Within 40 minutes, he was out of bed, and within a couple of hours, the pain was gone. When the Holy Spirit speaks to you, it's an experience that's worth all the gold in the world. It's another moment where 'the peace of God surpasses all understanding.'

The Source of Visions

Spiritual sight is developed through faith and openness. The more we know His ways, the better my sight. Good seed comes from the Lord and is intended to lead us to a fruitful experience. New business opportunities for goodness come from the seed of God's visions.

Committees don't birth good visions. They come to individuals. Some people call it their gut. Others call it their intuition. Yet, they come to the heart and soul. Depending on the emotional garden of your heart, they can have a powerful impact on you and your calling in life and business. The strength of committees is to think logically, using experiences, knowledge, and judgment. Visions come as revelations to us. As pastor Paul Zink says, *"Revelation Supersedes Calculation."*

While visions see beyond logic and into the future, most visions die in the battleground of the mind without capturing your imagination or the imagination of others. This is the challenge of the beaten down path, the rocky soil, and the thorny soil. For some people, it becomes merely the training ground for future receptivity of the vision. It is a vision that becomes reality in the marketplace, home, family, nation, or personal life, affecting millions of lives.

God is the giver of visions for His long-term purposes. Godly visions usually come in a time of humility, searching, or openness. There should be no false idols, wrong motives or selfishness before us. Remember Ray Kroc who sat in the parking lot that morning in San Bernardino? He was a humble man who saw a vision that the Mc-

Donald brothers could not embrace because they were worn down from the rocks and thorns.

Still, God had a plan for Ray Kroc, J.C. Penney, Billy Graham, and Mother Teresa, as well as for you and millions of others. If your heart is open to Him and more fertile than your old barren mindset, then He has a vision waiting for you. Paul Cuny, author of Secrets of the Kingdom Economy, says, *"He's not called Creator by chance. He created the heavens, earth, and each of us, enthused to create through us with the visions/dreams seeds He plants in our heart and soul."*

Through our faith, trust, and God's calling, we are retained in His seed. Instead of falling prey to the unproductive soils, our attitude needs to be positive. We need to have the belief that our vision is going to multiply—that we will overcome and persevere. Our goal is to sustain us through the hard, rocky, thorny times. It is about faith. In fact, nothing long-lasting happens without faith.

Isaiah 30:18 (NIV)

__Yet the Lord longs to be gracious to you;__
__therefore he will rise up to show you compassion.__
__For the Lord is a God of justice.__
__Blessed are all who wait for him!__

Reaching the Good Soil

Can you imagine the issues Abraham, Noah, and Moses went through to be faithful? The Word is telling us to hold on to the vision and there will be multiple returns. In fact, the Bible says that there will be a thirty fold, sixty fold or a hundredfold return on your investment, enterprise, marriage, or family.

Howard Schultz, Chairman of Starbucks writes, *"When you've got a dream or vision, you need to dream big. The bigger the dream, the more it will sustain you during the trials."* As an advisor to businesses, we encourage you to seek confirmation from other men and women of wisdom. This helps you determine whether your dream is of God and within your calling or whether it is rooted in your selfish desires to make money and achieve notoriety.

Zig Ziglar likens knowing our calling to taking a train *"You know a train is good, if it's on track. But, if it's not on a track it doesn't go very far."* We are created to be on His right track. It is critical that we know what His track is. Then, we simply need to hold on to it through the rough times and good times because they will come.

The mystery is that you can actually find the good soil when you accept your trials and tests with a joyful heart. We all face them in one way or another. The trial maybe from the world, but the test is from the Lord. The question is, *"How long will you hang in there to find success?"*

Never Give Up!

Dave Ramsey, the renowned financial expert, who often appears on national radio and TV shows, provides the tough financial advice. He learned and earned it by a humbling *"school-of-hard-knocks degree."* In his earlier years, he overextended himself in the real estate business and lost it all. But experiencing the rocky soil developed his character and prepared him for the next challenge. Today, Dave's national organization of 200 staff members is teaching and educating more than 100,000 people about how to effectively eliminate debt.

Dave Ramsey went from being very rich to being totally bankrupt. This happened for a reason. Through the pain, he found peace with Jesus and vowed to help others avoid debt. Participation in his Financial Peace University workshop is up 68 percent this year, and has helped people get out of debt for almost 20 years. More than three million people listen to his show every week on 325 radio stations. Now, his show also comes to television on the Fox Business News Network.

Truly successful people are bigger than their problems. What some would consider obstacles, they see as stepping-stones. Because Dave failed in the rocky and thorny soil of real estate, many are now blessed through him. When we seek God, He takes us from darkness to the light. Darkness represents confusion, failure or pain. Light is the path that gleams bright through a clear vision. No matter the storms, the peace of God lights your way.

> *"Life is like a camera, what you focus*
> *on will sharpen and develop"*
> BRIG HART, CO-FOUNDER OF USA ASSOCIATION

Turnarounds Abound

Doug Weiss was born in thorny soil. Conceived out of wedlock, he never met his father. As a good looking and smooth talking young man, he pursued the ladies. The seed of lust gripped his heart and soul until the day he finally surrendered to Christ.

Today, he is a top-selling author who has written 15 books on sex addiction and good marriage relationships. He's a gifted counselor and businessman who oversees a staff that strives to change people's lives. You may have seen him on Oprah or in the media answering questions and winning over the audiences.

Likewise, Zig Ziglar was a super charged salesman that could not consistently keep it together. As one of thirteen children from the small town of Yazoo, Mississippi, he lost his father when he was only nine years old. While he was good at his profession, he went from job to job trying to find greener pastures. His housekeeper led him to the Lord, and it turned his life around. For more than 40 years, he helped salesmen and executives *"get it together."* Unbelievably, in all of those years, he has never solicited a speaking engagement.

When John took a group to visit his office, the 85 year-old legend showed us pictures of that housekeeper and 20 others on his *"Wall of Gratitude"* because of their profound influence on his life. He recently passed away but spoke nationally and was still writing three new books a year to add to his collection of twenty-six already completed. He's been a friend of Presidents and CEOs as well as an inspiration to millions. Zig's adversity training in rocky soil prepared him to find his purpose in giving to others. His favorite saying was, *"If you help enough people get what they want, they will help you find what you want."* Sounds like the Golden Rule.

Another example of a businessman that experienced a dramatic turnaround in life is Patrick Morley. In the 1980s, he was a top commercial real estate developer in Florida. If fact, Pat was one of John's first CEO clients in Orlando. What we did not know, nor did he, was that he would come close to bankruptcy six years later.

As a smart and suave professional, Pat always looked like he stepped out of GQ magazine. But his heart carried the legacy of a grandfather who had abandoned his father when he was only two years old. Eventually, a real estate market down turn allowed the Lord to take deeper control and alter Pat's life. The Lord began an inner healing process. He gave Pat the passion to teach other men to become better husbands, fathers, and leaders.

The 'soil' experiences led him to write Man in the Mirror, a book, which has sold over three million copies. With a staff of 50 leaders and teachers, his ministry now reaches thousands of men and leaders around the country and internationally.

Good soil is found after persevering through the difficult soils in your past. By loving and giving to others, you begin to dig deep into the rich and abundant soil of life. In fact, the best instructor to alcoholics is the person who has experienced it firsthand and beat it. The Bible says the road of this world is broad and leads to destruction, but the path to righteousness is narrow. Believe it or not, He is quietly shepherding and ordering our steps.

Getting to the good soil can be rough whether you are called to build a multi-billion dollar business or run an orphanage in the mountains of Peru. Being a financial millionaire on earth or a spiritual millionaire by laying up treasures in heaven is a tough journey, but it's worth it.

> *"At the heart of faithfulness*
> *is an attitude of self-sacrifice."*
>
> — PASTOR RUSS AUSTIN

Is The Good Soil Good?

Did Jesus mean that you would finally reach the best soil, true success, if you just persevere? Or, in order to reach the good soil, must you break through the beaten down soil of your heart and remove the stones from rocky soil? Does it require you to pull up the thorns and weeds while constantly tilling the soil?

Consider this: It could be that good soil is already within you. You may simply need to remove the hard soil of your heart by breaking it up and laying a new path. The crushed rocks could actually lay a new foundation for your new business or ministry.

The band, known as Rascal Flatts, sings the song God Bless the Broken Road. Attempting to grow on the hard, thorny, or rocky paths is often a trial we don't cherish. But God has a wonderful plan, which is seldom straight or easy. A line from the song is, *"Others were just a northern star pointing me to you."* It was the Lord that used the northern star to lead the three kings to find the baby Jesus. We believe that's His plan for all of us.

Jesus still waits for us to discover the rich secrets of the Kingdom. If his purpose is making us a successful leader, God is patient. He never gives up on us. One thing for sure is this: We cannot do it alone. We need His grace and guidance.

The Seed Words of God

If you read the Word with spiritual eyes and pray, you realize that the seed is actually the Spirit of God. It is His seed that grows within our hearts, casts the vision, and motivates us to succeed. His seed is His word and plan for you. God grows the seed if it is planted in the right soil and nurtured with care. He is the multiplier.

In our world, words are the most powerful tools for all mankind. Words are God's tools for creation. He spoke the world into existence. Since we are created in the image and likeness of God, words are also our tools. The words you use are containers of thoughts, visions, knowledge, information, inspiration, ideas, directions, and commands.

Words of love build relationships and touch the heart and human spirit. They bring healing and compassion. Words of knowledge enlighten, cast visions, and promote hope and promise. Creative words are the source of inventions, energy, and economic exchange. However, words of hate spawn pain, prejudice, resentment, and war. Negative words drain energy and bring discouragement.

Words of Inspiration

The Bible is referred to as the inspired Word of God, given by the Holy Spirit to the authors. This is a critical truth for businessmen and women. If we are committed to the Lord's service above all other wants, with our spiritual eyes, we can see the depth of the Lord's purpose for us. All around the world, God is trying to speak—plant seeds—in every one of us. His seeds show us what we are to do and where we are to go. His Spirit wants to work mightily in and through us.

The seed that becomes a flowering tree is loaded with explosive power, nutrients, and energy. Its sole purpose is to grow and multiply. Only God knows how many apples will come from a small seed planted in good soil and properly nurtured. At the same time, only God knows if a husband's seed will create a precious child within his wife's womb. The power of a seed is ready to burst forward into new life when placed in the right soil or circumstance.

Mankind was created in His image as God spoke the world into existence. He spoke in the Spiritual realm to make things happen in the physical.

Spoken or read, words penetrate our hearts like seeds. They grow or die depending on the receptivity of our heart—our soil. In fact, your words and the meaning behind them are the most powerful tools of influence for all of mankind.

"Your words can bring life or death"

The words and thoughts of the Bible inspire us and align us with God's purpose and plan. He also works mysteriously through our relationships—the messengers He sends us. But first, we need to remove the rocks and thorns all around us. By preparing our hearts for His seed, we can be ready for real change and success. In fact, God is in control of the blessings and is waiting for our proper response. He wants us to be unashamed and unhindered in following His plan for our lives.

Conrad Hilton once said that it was *"through my faith in God, my prayers and seeking Him that I came out of bankruptcy to build the Hilton Hotel chain."* His is an incredible story of how his public prayers and faith affected our nation. The founder of our National Day of Prayer, he inspired people by his faith. Most importantly, he openly displayed his relationship with God for the whole nation to see in the national publications of his day.

The Burden, Giving It All Away

Bill Gates has been declared the richest man in the world seven times. He does not care anymore and would just as well forget the fame that comes with wealth. His responsibility today is much harder than building a huge company.

The Lord gave me this phrase years ago when I wrote my first book and it's worth repeating...

> ### *"True Wealth is not a measure of success but of responsibility."*
> #### JOHN BEEHNER

If you don't respond to what God is directing you to do, it can become a very heavy burden, no matter whether you are listening for Him or not. Bill and his team have studied the results of the millions given away by the Andrew Carnegie and John D. Rockefeller Foundations. Rockefeller often said he felt gifted by God to make money. Many have attributed the Rockefeller's as being the key to saving millions from malaria, tuberculosis and diphtheria around the world.

While Bill and Melinda Gates have given away billions to education and many worthy causes, they have not been as successful as they want in Africa and many nations eradicating AIDS. It has been a deep passion of theirs. Is this their thorny soil? Is it possible AIDS is a spiritual disease, not to be eradicated by drugs but by prayer and the spirit of God?

Gift of Sight from the Giver of Light

Dave Browne, is the former CEO of Lenscrafters, the national retail chain and seller of eye apparel. Frustrated and bored in a Christian workshop one day, he walked outside with his Bible to sit at a park bench. Concerned about the business and numerous issues, he sought the Lord and as he opened his Bible—a scripture seemed to jump off the page and captivate him.

Luke 7:21 — *At that very time Jesus cured many who had diseases, sicknesses and evil spirits, and gave sight to many who were blind.*

Dave immediately saw a vision to create a program that would be known as the *"The Gift of Sight."* The concept ran for many years of giving away used eyeglasses to the needy in the USA and many nations of the world. They created traveling caravans of employees and doctors examining and fitting people with glasses that most had never experienced before.

It inspired the employees of Lenscrafters and employee turn over dropped by 75% and profits grew dramatically. Employees no longer saw their work as a job but as a mission. Dave eventually went on to become CEO of Family Christian Stores where he used some of the same concepts to build teamwork, unity and sense of calling.

Driven by the Spirit

Maybe you have heard of the Cecil B. De Mille the spectacular movie director of the 1950's era. He hired Charlton Heston in two movies that are significant in our culture, .The Ten Commandments and Ben Hur.

In filming Ben Hur they had to teach Charlton Heston how to ride in a chariot holding the reins of two racing horses in the coliseum against other experienced chariot drivers in competitive races. After his extensive training Charlton told Cecil, *"I have mastered the driving the chariot but I have one problem."*

Cecil said, *"Now, what could that be?"*

Charlton said, *"I can do my best, but I am not sure I can win."*

Cecil laughed and said, *"You do the driving with all your heart, and I will make sure you win in the end."*

That is the same message the Lord is trying to get to us. We should be obedient following our heart to do our best and He will take care of the success part and make sure we win when we are supposed to.

In Luke, 8:14 Jesus said, *"For everyone who exalts himself will be humbled and whoever humbles himself will be exalted"* (by God).

"Money is great servant
but a horrible master."

BRIG HART, CO-AUTHOR AND CO-FOUNDER OF USA ASSOCIATION

USA Association "To take back the USA"

Brig cherishes the spirit of our founding fathers to sacrifice who created our Freedom to pursue our own happiness, our Constitution, Bill of Rights and in opposition to Tyranny. American Freedom has a set of standards that our founders derived from the Ten Commandments. They set up a judicial system to protect and allow for consequences for those violating our moral rights to pursue happiness.

The creation of USA Association is not about Brig Hart, direct selling or MLM, but our mutual sacrifice to help our nation return to its greatness. Too many of our fellow Americans are misguided to believe that subsidies, government spending and control will make a better society. Thomas Jefferson said, *"My reading of history convinces me that most bad government results from too much government."*

God gave us *"free will"* as the cornerstone of freedom and expects us to take self-initiative, not be dependent on government. We are called to use our gifts and talents individually and collectively to improve and grow as mothers, fathers and providers for our families, businesses and ministries. Government is meant to serve us not control us. Poor people don't need a hand out but a hand up.

God has protected America through its calling and purposes. He has used us to be a light onto the world. We can't afford to become a socialist nation and spiritually bankrupt like so many others have done. The world needs our spirit and leadership for freedom.

"I am in my final chapters seeking to do what I am called to do. I believe I was born and raised through adversity for a time such as this. The Lord has given me a vision for building an Army of Believers who want to see Biblical values and the Character of

our Founders, restored in our nation. It requires a united voice of conservative Americans who will speak with passion to cry out for Faith, Family and Free Enterprise to be restored and championed in the USA. The Lord will allow us continue to falter, if good people sit by, watch and do nothing. We must stand up for what is right, using our voice, votes and pocket books.

Some how God has give this little stature of mine, the passion and ability to inspire and motivate people to take action. I pray that it is still His plan in this calling for the Lord to help bring back our nation to His standards. I hope to be in my ultimate good soil with good fruit from all we do. I pray you will join us."

WWW.USAASSOC.COM

5 Keys to Staying in Good Soil

1. Staying on Course, open to the plan as it unfolds

2. Loving and giving *"Love covers a multitude of sins"* — 1Peter 4:8

3. Be a Doer of the Word, not just hearer — James 1:22

4. Walking your talk, being in the Potter Hands

5. Being the Student Teacher — Luke 10:37

Where does Good Soil come from ?

We have a favorite quote that offers so much insight on this.

> ***"Wisdom comes from Good Judgment***
> ***Good Judgment comes from experience***
> ***And Experience comes from bad decisions"***

So where does Good Soil come from? It comes from bad decisions of fermented soil, human excrement and decayed matter that has been broken down over time through the struggles and frustrations in your life. In other words, it comes from your failures, dead projects and experiences that have fermented over the years...bad decisions in your life of risk taking to accomplish something. All of this has become your best soil filled with your own fertilizer of experiences and mistakes.

The Lord can use this Good Soil and knows how you will be most effective with your search to gain His wisdom and insight you cannot find alone or mature without His help. You and He are partners to accomplish His plan not your own. We believe that Steve Jobs and even Bill Gates have come to this realization that they are called to something much greater than themselves. It's the mission you discover in the process in finally reaching Good Soil.

Good Soil is a Clear Understanding
Wisdom beyond this age to serve His greater mission

CHAPTER 10

The Secret to True Wealth

When it comes to being a living legend and achieving your true wealth, why do some people succeed and others fail? How do successful business people flush out God's visions, thoughts, and ideas that He's placed in their heart and soul?

We understand that both natural and human seeds grow to reproduce additional seed for the next cycle or generation. Part of your mission is to plant your spiritual seed within your employees, customers, vendors, suppliers, community and all interested parties. Display your spirit and enthusiasm through your vision as well as your persistence to get the job done, build your organization, and serve others.

The overall plan is to share your passion and build esprit de corps to win together. People want to follow leaders of faith and heart-felt vision. By speaking, loving, and caring for people, you are like a teacher and salesman that help your team accomplish the mission together. You are their inspiration, because they could have never done it alone. The Word says, *"We who teach will be judged more strictly."* You are held to a higher standard, but reap greater rewards.

Then you must move from not just visionary but to leader. People want to follow leaders who cast the vision and then delegate, involve and trust them to help accomplish the mission.

Al Lopus, Founder of the Best Christian Workplace Institute who evaluates 100's of companies and ministries on a regular basis through employee surveys says productivity is at its highest when employees are *"engaged"* not just *"satisfied."* Engagement is about trust and involvement where they feel they are contributing through their ideas and decisions to move together as a winning team accomplishing something greater than they can do by themselves. Ultimately, they feel ownership.

In their minds they say, *"This is my organization and I am proud to be a contributing partner."*

Levels of Transition in Business

How much does knowledge and application of faith affect your business success?

How effective are you as a person of faith?

Read these and decide.

1. Unconscious Incompetent Beaten Down Soil

I don't know what I don't know. I don't recognize or have confidence in my self to undertake visions or ideas that come to my mind. Yet, if your faith is small as a mustard seed, you still have hope.

2. Unconscious Competent Rocky Soil

I see my self as successful but I don't have the faith and belief in my self or in the vision/idea to sustain it. I love the idea but the circumstances are too tough to handle.

3. Conscious Incompetent Thorny Soil

I know what I don't know. I recognize I have a lot to learn and need more faith to fight discouragement to get me through the ups, down and trails. I will draw on the encouragement of the Lord or others and do my best to preserve.

4. Conscious Competent Good Soil

I am humble and believe we have the know how and talent to achieve success. It's not about me but a greater mission birth in me to accomplish success beyond my expectations.

The Secret to the Kingdom of God is found in the Parable of the Sower. For some it is starting on the Beat Down path where is a good idea is beyond their reach or belief. Then as they grow in self confidence or faith, visions/ideas from the Lord come during the Rocky Soil of their mind, yet the risk is worth taking. Then as their mind grows to Thorny, they learn to preserve, become more humble and yet aggressive enough to live, grow and advance to Good Soil. For many people this is God's plan to take them through these stages of growth and have to accomplish His greatest mission for their True Wealth.

Others may start in Rocky soil or Thorny soil and others enthusiastically begin in Good Soil. Good soil is mission driven but not free of rocky or thorny experiences. But at this point of experience they are better and more experienced to handle the down turns.

	Incompetence	Competence
Unconscious	I don't know, what I don't know.	I'm successful but I don't know why.
Conscious	I know, what I don't know.	I know why and how to be successful.

Less = More

**"Less of me, more of my people
and more of the Lord
gives me more wisdom."**

ERIC SWENSON, COACH AND AUTHOR

Sharing and Inspiring

- Howard Schultz, of Starbucks, built success around his vision. Even today his enthusiasm is contagious, which inspires his employees to be both friendly and motivated.

- Herb Kelleher, founder and former CEO of Southwest, was intense, humorous, and genuine in sharing the spirit of his vision with his people.

- Sam Walton was a great showman who lifted the spirit of his people every time he visited a store.

- Clark Johnson, former CEO who had a tremendous impact on the growth of Pier One Imports, claimed that he loved to share the vision of Pier One as he talked with employees. He said that sharing the mission with his people was like Vitamin C, *"because it dissipates in the system, people can't get too much of it."* He ingrained in them to love customer complaints because that's how they learned to do better in serving them.

On our way to success, the crux of the journey is to give back to others like God gave to us. Any visionary's mission is to live on and to be a legacy. But what kind of legacy are your leaving? What seeds are you sowing? Better yet, are you sowing with God's seeds?

In church, you hear people use the expression that they are going to sow into a certain ministry with their time or treasures. It works the same in business. After all, every business is a ministry and every ministry a business.

In the scriptures, it says our words are like sparks of fire that can corrupt, burn, and spread like never-ending flames of destruction. At the same time, our words can produce new growth of enthusiasm, positive energy and commitment to bare new fruit.

> ### *"God spoke the world into existence and He gave us the same power in our tongue for His creative good."*

It all comes back to the power of your words. Are you a giver or a taker? Do you establish a culture of enthusiasm where the spirit seed of God can flourish? The purpose of a business is not to make a profit but to serve the needs of others in an environment where they can grow and minister to one another.

Evil wins when that does not happen and success withers like a dying plant. Too many leaders speak encouragement to people's faces, yet ridicule them behind their backs. Our mission is to encourage and speak the best into people in order to accomplish our calling and honor Him.

Sacrifice is a responsibility

Ever since Adam and Eve, God through out the whole Old Testament has called man to provide animal sacrifices to atone for his sins. When the Lord sent his son Jesus to die for the sins of the world he changed the game of life. Yet, we believe every one of us lives and dies as a sacrifice for those who come after us. While we have stood on the backs of our parents, leaders and fellowman.

Everyone who dies, young or old leaves a mark or sends a message for the rest of us to avoid a mistake, find an answer or cure, be faithful through adversity, be a role model, make a change or conduct research to make a better world. Jesus paid the greatest price and faced a humiliation that few of us will even approach. If a business owner is struggling he or she is in the midst of a sacrifice.

Our Mission in life and business is to:

1. **Be willing to sacrifice** us for our greater purpose.

2. **Welcome a chance to sacrifice** for our neighbors, our customers and employees.

3. **Be obedient in our sacrifice** to serve God's greater calling in us.

Just like Jesus did. He is our role model.

> *"A Christianity that costs nothing*
> *is worth nothing."*
> —Pastor Ricky Roberts

Sowing Bad Seed

Part of our struggle is our 'stinkin thinkin' or the 'fears' we have hidden in our soul. Ultimately, we believe it is fear that drives so many away from pursuing the real calling for success in their lives. Fears can grip us and becomes the rocks, weeds and thorns that choke the visions we receive.

The even deeper truth is that we all inherit physical traits and tendencies of our ancestors. The same is true of the pains and sins of our parents that the Bible says are passed on from generation to generation. A friend of mine told me recently that he had, with the Lord's direction, overcome the life-long curse of his father being an abusive parent.

As a teenager, both Brig and I mouthed off a few times to our parents. But I will never forget one particular time that my dad yelled at me to get to my room. He was so mad that he practically broke down my locked bedroom door and came in to whip me. I will never forget that incident, because as I lay there crying, I promised myself that I would never lose my temper with my kids. Guess what? I did. I regretted it and sought forgiveness, many times. Thankfully, the Lord has delivered me from that curse, but my kids may still be affected. Still, because of His unfailing love, the Lord is the healer of such words and pains.

The Deceiver of God's Plan

There is an enemy that seeks to thwart God's purpose for your life. It is the mission of the deceiver, Satan, to trap us in the thorns of self-centered thinking. Pride, egotism, greed, and arrogance act like a cancer to destroy any hope of true success. Satan's deceit caused Adam and Eve to vanish from the Garden of Eden. As a result we are all born with self-will and the self-centered thinking disease. If we continue to buy into the lies of evil, we will also be effectively neutralized or diverted from God's greater plan.

God is a spirit of love, truth, and life. He is invisible to the human eye, as is Satan. God works through love and Satan works through hate. Satan wants to demoralize our faith and play the 'bad memory tapes of our early childhood or fears and past failures' over and over again in your minds. If he can't kill us, he will divert us by keeping us too busy or skeptical to receive the seed of God in our troubled hearts. It's basically guerilla warfare, creating confusion, skirmishes, and doubt—the same tactics as al-Qaeda.

I was leaving a restaurant, and a man was telling three other men loudly, *"God is good and the devil is bad."*

My associate with me said, *"And man is in between."* That means—we have a choice.

"The Battle is not ours," says the Lord

Have You Got the Mustard?

The Parable of the Mustard Seed is referenced at least six times in scripture. Jesus said that faith is like a mustard seed, which even though one and two millimeters in diameter can become the biggest tree in the garden. The tree grows so large that it even provides places for birds to perch.

In Matthew, 17:20 , if Jesus says, *"Truly I tell you have faith as small as a mustard seed, you can move mountains."*

- Orville Redenbacher had faith that his special quality pop-corn could be sold in more outlets than just his roadside stand in Indiana. He didn't realize that his dream would create a new industry.

- Mary Kay wasn't trying to create a giant company. Instead, she sought to exercise her faith in God that she could help other women after being dumped by her old company.

- Ray Kroc wanted to save his hurting milk shake mixer business, not forever change the restaurant industry. It was a question of survival. Yet, he had the faith and willingness to take the risk to visit the McDonald brothers halfway across the country in the 1950s.

Does the Lord want you to accomplish what seems to be a very small vision? Can a simple idea become much bigger than you think?

God can use you regardless of who you are or where you've been. Whether you are a high school dropout or have a Master's Degree in business. God is no stranger to performing miracles. If you don't believe me, go visit your local nursery and buy a pack of mustard seeds. Consider how something so small can grow so large. God can make His vision a reality in your life even if your faith is small like a mustard seed—not much bigger than a period on this paragraph.

Bottom Line Fruit and Profits

Linda Rios Brook spent many years in network television working with ABC, CBS, and NBC as the president and general manager of affiliates in Texas, Florida, and Minnesota. In 1991, she found herself in the middle of frenzy in both the secular and Christian media about a Bible study she led in the evenings. Her options were to resign or stop teaching. She decided to resign her high paid position from the NBC affiliate in Minneapolis rather than hide her faith.

The following year she, along with her husband, Larry, and a handful of investors, bought an independent television station out of bankruptcy in St. Paul, MN, for $3.2 million.

They struggled the first year. Some board members felt strongly about airing the Rush Limbaugh TV show, carried nationally at the time, to build their audience base. But to carry the show the producers required that they also had to air the Jerry Springer show. Linda rejected the idea because of the 'family fights' the show emphasized. Later, she reluctantly, decided to carry the Springer show to get Limbaugh, without a sure confirmation from the Lord.

But before the Jerry Springer show was to air, she received a vision from the Lord to involve local counseling agencies and ministries. She ran at the bottom of each show, the tag line 'if you are in crisis and need help call...' The switch boards lit up with thousands of calls every night. As many as 30,000 calls a month for six years. Thousands found help and many found Christ.

Bottom line, the results from the Jerry Springer counseling effort bore more fruit than 75% of the churches in America. The station became very profitable and seven years later, they sold it to a large media conglomerate for $52.5 million net to the shareholders.

Getting to the Bottom Line

God's principles revolve around relationships. At the center of the eternal model of success is our investment in Relationship Capital. None of us can buy our way into heaven. You can give away millions of dollars, but if you only do it for tax reasons or with a resentful heart, it has no rewards in heaven.

The Parable of the Sower calls you to use your gifts and talents to overcome fear, obstacles, thorns, and all the difficult situations in life. By doing so, you are then able to hear God and plant the seed of His word in fertile soil that will be tilled, fertilized, and aerated by your sweat and tears.

In order to uncover the Secret to the Kingdom of God, we must learn to overcome obstacles brought on in the trials we face. The 'crushing rocks' and the 'prickly thorns' are often the words of pessimistic people we encounter. Many successful organizations and individuals have contributed greatly to mankind by persevering despite their obstacles.

Habitat for Humanity is a beautiful example. After experiencing the thorny soil of marital turmoil, Millard Fuller and his wife followed a vision to impact millions around the world. Dr. Jonas Salk, who in 1955 discovered the vaccine for polio after years of experimentation with as many 64,000 patients, has helped reshape the world. Billy Graham and Oprah Winfrey have spread the gospel in different ways while enduring the fire of criticism. Oprah affects people every day and she attempts to plant goodness in their hearts rather than dwell on the negative things about life. She's recorded as saying, *"Jesus is my inspiration,"* so we won't judge her destiny after this life.

Billy and Oprah have modeled in different ways what Jesus said are the two greatest commandments:

1. **Love God with all your heart** (by spreading the gospel).

2. **Love your neighbor** (by modeling godly behavior and passion for people).

*"The highest use of capital
is not to make more money,
but to make money do more
for the betterment of life."*

—HENRY FORD, FOUNDER OF FORD MOTOR COMPANY

ROI and ROE

Part of God's plan is to receive a Return on Investments (ROI), but He also wants a Return on Eternity (ROE). What we're doing on Earth will have an impact on eternity. In fact, that is where our mission and final destination lies. It says in the Word, *"Whoever can be trusted with little can be trusted with much."* (Luke 16:10)

That crystallizes the message of the Parable of the Sower, as well as the Parable of the Talents. It continues, *"If you've not been trustworthy in handling worldly wealth, who will trust you with true riches?"* In other words, if we're not on the right path, and we are not nourishing God's seed for His eternal purpose and calling, we will struggle in the rocky and thorny places (with or without the money).

The fact of the matter is even if you don't know God, you can learn from your mistakes and gravitate to the things you're good at. Tom Watson, developer of IBM said, *"Good companies just make mistakes faster,"* and therefore, learn faster. Many of us have said to the Lord, *"What is it that You are really trying to get me to do here? How do I do it? And, how do I do it effectively?"* The moral of the story is: Do what you're called and entrusted to do. If you sincerely trust Him to be leading you, He will work through you step by step. He loves the journey, just like you like playing youth baseball and He will be with you and attend each game to cheer you on as his own son. He says in His word *"He will never leave of forsake you."*

Though God gave us free will, He is calling us to walk a deeper path and trusting us to accomplish His plan. No matter how tough it is or how big the test can be, God entrusts us to persevere through the whole journey in order to know true success. He is our source. The truth is, *"No branch can bear fruit by itself; neither can a branch bear fruit unless you remain in me and my words remain in you."* (John 15:4-5)

You may not even know God. However, it is possible to understand His ways of Relationship Capital and build a business success here on earth. The problem is, as they say, you can't take it with you. Without a relationship with God, you cannot get to heaven, even if you follow His principles for success on earth.

The Jim Penney Legacy

J.C. Penney was an incredibly successful businessman. He learned Biblical business principles from his father, who was a pastor. His first three stores, beginning in the mining town of Kemmerer, Wyoming, were called the Golden Rule Stores. Within 15 years, his business grew so rapidly that he built or acquired 350 stores to the chain. At that point, left the company he had founded, because he thought he had the *"Midas Touch,"* to turn anything into a success.

But Jim's next vision failed, largely from the stock market crash of 1929 where he lost 90% of his personal wealth. So at 54, suffering from shingles and depression, he believed he was on his deathbed in a hospital in Battle Creek, Michigan. In shear pain and depression, he reached out to God again and again asking for forgiveness. This prompted a deeply spiritual encounter that caused him to surrender to Christ, anew. The Lord showed him that He was growing the J.C. Penney Company, not himself. He realized he was just a vessel of the Lord to serve people and customers for His greater purposes.

This became his secret to success—yielding completely to God's plan. From that encounter he discovered His greatest plan of ministering and coaching other businessmen. He was an inspiration for thousands. Instead of dying he went on to live to be 95 re-energized and healed for a great and new undertaking.

His plan for your life and pursuing His calling, will change your life through peace, love, and joy, you will receive for the journey. The Lord works in the hearts of businessmen and women who receive His vision, whether they know him or not. But the Creator of heaven and earth is not gauging your success based on financial merits. Instead, your contribution to the Kingdom is grounded in your obedience to His calling and plan. In fact, He is laying up treasures in heaven for the work we do on earth.

"Winners are losers who got back up."

Stages of the Parable of the Sower

Soil Condition	Mindset and Openness
Hard and Beaten Down Soil and Path	Pride, Ignorant, Stubborn, lack of faith, selfish, selective hearer, fear
Rocky Soil	Faith and fear battle, shallow thinking
Thorny Soil	Attacked by deceit, lack of trust. Becomes a battle for survival with growth
Good Soil	Mission, humility, obedience, trust, clay in Potter's hands, His will to be done for His motives

False God of Accomplishment

God placed a DNA in the soul of every man to accomplish something significant or as some might describe as 'make your mark' on His world. That passion causes many men to 'chase success,' without full discernment as to their calling and timing. There is sowing time and harvest time. Many of us are trying to push forward faster than the Lord's plan.

Every step is a learning experience. Adversity is about building our character and resolve to make things work.

Getting through the different soils of the Parable of the Sower is not always about accomplishment but obedience. There are times when the Lord wants us to learn lessons that will help future generations.

I have counseled many entrepreneurs who say that their greatest need is capital. There is a *"worldly perspective"* that they need the capital to buy their way to success. Capital is a good tool but spent on the wrong inventory or wrong location it can take a business down.

So many small business start-ups and innovators come in search of equity capital and connections with the potential investors—most come with their heart set on making a deal. The Lord is calling us to want to grow and to be dependent on Him to open the doors in His timing—not our own.

Calvin Bryant, at 19 had his own Internet development business with as many as 20 employees and associates. He was a pioneer, genius and entrepreneur on a pace faster than his maturity, knowledge and ability to lead or manage people could be sustained. Fifteen years later, with a hundred clients he can now maintain his business with just six associates. In the maturing process of the School of Hard Knocks, he says one of his greatest lessons was, *"The Lord taught me, I had to learn I could not always sprint and there was a practical time to jog and even a time I had to learn to walk in my business pace."*

Being a Successful Failure

Why would God call you to a business that is not successful? Well, let me ask you this question: If your son wants to become a doctor, wouldn't you suggest that he take chemistry or human anatomy in school? Why? You'd do it to test his interest, passion and level of commitment to what he would need to learn. It would also allow himself to test his interest level and abilities. God tests us like we would test our son.

In other words, your purpose is to help your son discover his real talents, which may be in a different field of study. So, when it comes to your unsuccessful business venture, was God calling you to this business or was it your personal desires that you wanted Him to bless. Or was the Lord allowing you to experience sales, manufacturing or graphic design that will serve you well in your bigger assignment that you cannot envision yet. God loves a failure that admits his mistakes and tries again but this time is better prepared and wiser.

In church this morning a lady of prayer, told the congregation that the Lord had said to her, *"I will take your failures and turn them into something beautiful...a beautiful crown. You cannot buy my love. Keep pressing forward and let go the things of the past."*

Kingdom Boot Camp

God can use the hard, rocky or thorny soil to break your will. The Lord never wanted us to be on our own, but He allowed Adam and Eve and all of us who followed to experience pain, good and evil with out Him. Why? To teach us—to give us a chance to surrender and find the Truth of His ways.

That is the same purpose of the military boot camp or prison to break your will and train you to become obedient—it's basic training—to be set free of your own will. 'True Freedom' is found in Him—unselfishness, without lust, greed, drugs and false gods. We are to surrender and follow His will and the plan he has for your life and mine.

Thomas O'Galin found gold in scrap iron. Thomas, a strong willed Irishman struggled for nearly 15 years with alcohol until he discovered Alcoholic Anonymous, his first boot camp experience. His big wake up call came after he barely escaped prison time. You can image his rocky experiences in his boot camp. With a bad economy, he lost his job.

Then one night he received a vision to start a new business. God gave him a 'vision seed' of the old TV show called Sanford and Sons, popular in the 1980's. He had had some success in selling scrap metal before so he quickly grasped the idea. Using his old pick up truck he has been able to earn a living and build a business picking up scrap metal and other things people call *"junk"* and reselling them for a profit.

My Journey is Now His plan

In 1994, when Herman Cain was president of Godfather Pizza, he also became the first black president of the 75-year-old National Restaurant Association. During his tenure, he testified before Congress on matters affecting America's 10 million restaurant workers. He has called for reform in the child labor laws to allow 16-year-olds to work past 7 p.m. on Fridays, since there is no school on Saturday.

Herman writes in his newest book, *"One of the keys to success in business is being happy with what you are doing, no matter what you earn. Success is not the key to happiness. Happiness is the key to success. If you love what you are doing, you will be*

CHAPTER 10 — TRUE WEALTH

successful. *Give God the glory. Throughout my life, I've looked to God for guidance, but He doesn't speak through a letter or a telephone. Your spirit has to be open to His voice. He has often guided me through my wife, my mother, my children, my friends, experiences or a Sunday-morning sermon."*

Little did he know he was heading into very rocky soil in 2006. He said, *"At that time, I heard three words that changed my life forever, two doctors told me I had colon and liver cancer. What went through my mind was, 'OK, Lord, if this is it, thank you for this wonderful life. I just pray that I don't suffer.' But when the doctor told me I had a 30 percent chance of survival, I had to start thinking, 'Well, maybe this is it.' But because of my faith, I wasn't afraid."*

"It's been more than six years since then. And guess what? I'm completely cancer-free! Cured!" Cain wrote. *"Why was I spared against those odds? God said, 'Not yet!' Did it have something to do with the Lord wanting me to survive so that I might help set this great nation of ours on its own path of recovery? I had achieved what I thought was my plan in life. My journey now is God's plan."*

You Are Being Chiseled

In Greek, the word character means, 'to chisel.' We all have rough spots that need a little chiseling. The process is painful, but it molds us and prepares us for a bigger and more meaningful calling. God measures your success by your obedience, perseverance, and willingness to give back to others. In fact, we have two tests to pass when our time is up on Earth.

1. **The God Test**—When you get to heaven, will you be greeted with, *"Well done, thy faithful servant?"* Or *"Why didn't you listen to me? I sent you people, small voices, and visions which you rejected."*

2. **The Fellow Man Test**—What will your fellow man say and think about you at your funeral? Who will come? What will be the thoughts in the hearts of those who came and those who didn't? Who will pray for your soul? Will you be missed? What will your legacy be?

The Creator Creates

We were all created to do the will of the Father. The Lord is so patient in waiting for us to get our acts together and He gives us multiple chances to come home. Good works are for the manifestation of the character of God; will of God, and the power of God. Noble acts of our own intention outside of these areas will not normally be fruitful in the long run.

Os Hillman, the author and speaker of Marketplace Leaders says, *"Is your plan a God idea or a good idea for God?"* John has asked that question of several entrepreneurs with multi-millionaire plans, most of which were FOR God rather than OF God. He is not interested in just being our inspiration—which comes from the word Spirit—but is actively in the center and leading us, giving us ideas and providing clues every step of the way. God's ideas bear fruit much greater than you as the business gardener can ever imagine on your own.

John has started three different ministry ideas for the Lord and then tried to get Him involved. While they were great ideas, they never lasted. That's why the Bible calls Him *"The Creator."* He comes up with the ideas and plans to use us to move the world forward by His great and long-term design. Our job is obedience, not creativity.

You could look at the four different soils of the Parable of the Sower as the Lord's way of testing you. How faithful will you be with your calling? All callings are in preparation for a bigger one if you have taken the risk and sacrifice to try to accomplish its purpose. While it may be about money in your mind, remember no scam artist makes money long term. True success without building relationships and trust will not succeed.

Jim Dismore, the former senior vice president of Wal-Mart, began with Sam Walton and his brother as they opened the third store and had a profound impact on their fast paced growth for the first 13 years. After he left, he felt the Lord revealed many powerful insights to him on true business success.

Here is one of the keys he shared with John years ago, *"The world's model for success is performance based with the focus on sales, cash flow, and productivity. That model cannot be effective without first being undergirded and built on the Relationship Model exemplified and taught by Jesus Christ."*

The Discerning Listener

Who do you think was the inventor of the television or the cell phone? It was our Creator. He works through individuals and mankind to develop many wondrous things. He even created the first wireless communication system. It has been called prayer for thousands of years. God's system works internationally, with no charge. But if your receiver is not tuned into the right frequency, you won't know whether you've gotten through.

That's where the deceiver is always trying to send his static of negative and skeptical thinking. The Bible uses the word discernment, which means separating falsehood from truth. Within the first three months of committing to the Lord, the Holy Spirit impressed on John's heart to pray for discernment. It has been a major part of his life. We urge you to pray for discernment as well.

God can use a risk taker who fails multiple times more than one who already perceives he is successful. Why? Because, *"Success is never permanent, failure is never final."* The Lord loves failures because those who fail are more prepared to pray harder, seek His help, build a stronger relationship with Him, walk in humility, and hopefully never give up.

Most importantly, the Lord never gives up on us and has no plans for our retirement. The word retirement was created by the Social Security system and does not appear in the Bible. The secret to true wealth is to get back up when you are knocked down. God has goodness waiting for all that pursue Him.

The Turning Point

Mike Schneider and his wife started a regional restaurant concept called The Loop in the 1980's. Mike's wife for years would preach to him about the Lord and he would just try to find ways to mock her. Mike's mother was a daughter of Baptist pastor and his dad was Jewish. So they decided to raise him by ignoring churches and synagogues. He had no faith in a God. But prayer groups targeted him. One day a high school friend called with a message from the Lord. It had a dramatic impact on him and after reading the book of John, he had a Holy Spirit encounter in his car.

He became a student of the Word and even held Bible Studies in his business. His heart became more and more open until he approached a group of men in a workshop about his dilemma. He felt he should sell his business to enter the ministry. After thorough questioning, the group advised him *"you are already in the ministry...through your business and your employees."* They suggested he consider creating a Chaplain program. So with help of the Chaplain of the NFL Jacksonville Jaguar team they recruited youth pastors to work part time in the restaurants to build relationships and minister to the needs of the employees.

A restaurant trade magazine thought is was novel idea and wrote an article on Mike's program for employees. The New York

<u>Times</u> picked up the article and wrote it's own piece in their Sunday addition.

More recently one of Mike's key supervisors, who has been considered an atheist and opposed to the Chaplain program was meeting with a new franchisee in North Carolina who asked how he could reduce employee turnover and create better chemistry among the staff. Surprising the same supervisor recommended he create a Chaplain program which had reduced turnover, and improved moral in their company owned stores. He said the Chaplains are well received and help people in their personal troubles.

Mike claims the Chaplain program is the decision he is most proud of in his 32 years of running the business. Mike said, *"I appreciate and need to make money, but helping our people become good citizens is very important and helping them fulfill their dreams is my heart. I am blessed to help people."* The bottom line is that his employee turnover is only 40% per year vs. as high as 400% average for the fast food industry nationally.

Going Full Cycle

Beaten down path—
hard headed and eating greasy bad food in college

Jordan Rubin at 19 experienced nausea, digestive distress, and an alarming weight loss of more than 80 pounds. Eventually, he was diagnosed with Crohn's Disease, a chronic digestive illness that affects the immune system. Wheelchair-bound and 104 pounds, one doctor's grim diagnosis was that it was *"the worst case of Crohn's"* he had ever seen and he did not expect Jordan to live.

Rocky Soil—rough times leads to desperate thinking

Fortunately, Jordan and his family—his support circle—were determined and sought more than 70 alternative nutritional therapies throughout the world after conventional medicine and numerous hospitalizations failed. His quest for answers concluded with a visit to a California nutritionist who simply told him he was not healthy because he was not following God's plan.

Thorny Soil—entangled thinking but captured the vision and opportunities to overcome the thorns/ obstacles

Touched by the Lord and inspired by this advice, Jordan voraciously studied hundreds of biblical references about living a healthy lifestyle. He changed his diet to whole foods consumed in biblical times: raw, organically grown whole grains, fruits, vegetables, and fermented dairy, grass fed beef and poultry. He also added a daily regimen of probiotics teeming with beneficial bacteria in soil-based organisms. After gaining 29 pounds in 40 days, Jordan knew he was finally on the right track. By his 21st birthday he was tipping the scales at more than 180 pounds, free of the digestive problems that had plagued him for years, and ready to restart his life.

Good Soil—being open to God's leading.

Becoming Clay in the Potter's Hands

Because Jordan was deeply moved by his restored health, he promised he would dedicate the rest of his life to sharing his health wisdom with the rest of the world and to transforming the health of the nation one life at a time. In 1999, he and his wife founded Garden of Life, now a leading whole foods nutrition company. The company's innovative products and commitment to efficacy quickly resounded with health conscious consumers and by 2004,

Garden of Life was named one of the fastest growing privately held companies by Entrepreneur Magazine and Inc. 500.

Determined to share his vision of health with as many people as possible, Jordan has written top selling books, such as The Maker's Diet, Great Physician's Rx Health series, Perfect Weight America and the Vitamin Code.

Die to self

The truth is that we need die to ourselves, for God to breath His richest new life into our businesses and knowing His calling. John 12:24 reads, *"Very truly I tell you, unless a kernel of wheat falls to the ground and dies, it remains only a single seed. But if it dies, it produces many seeds."* Only in the garden of Christ, can we produce a successful enterprise through the leading of the Lord.

Your vision, the seed that God has given you, cannot become a reality unless it is planted and dies to itself. Nourished by the good soil of God's love and power, that seed will blossom into a successful business or ministry that multiplies and bears much fruit.

Architect Robert Maurer said recently, "Jesus is sole source provider" (in construction terms means only service provider). We like that and took it one step further.

Jesus is our Soul Provider
ROBERT MAURER, AIA

Looking through my Father's eyes

So many of the lyrics of this popular hit song says what we are trying to share in this book. We hope you read it carefully because it's about perspective and attitude through our ups and downs of life, business and ministry. If can just surrender enough to the Lord your vision will be accelerate 100% and you can see what the Lord is doing through you.

The song is *"Through My Father's Eyes"* Written by: Holly Starr (she sings it), Chuck Butler, and Juan Otero.

Lyrics:

So many days I listened to the voice inside my head
Never thought that I'd be someone who could be misled
I wanted the mirror to show me something I could not see
Needed explanations for expectations I could never reach
I know I'm not the only one who's ever cried for help
And Jesus did for me what I could not do myself

He changed my life by changing my mind
He healed all that was broken inside
I'm loving what I can see with His spirit alive in me
I'm finding beauty for the first time
Looking through my Father's eyes
(Looking through my Father's eyes)

From what I see it looks like you don't
    like yourself too much
When I hear you talk it sounds like you
    just feel like giving up
I know it's hard to see through what this world will tell you
'Cause misconceptions and false reflections
    will never be the truth

Just know you're not the only one who's ever cried for help
Jesus loves you in ways that you cannot love yourself
I can see your freedom coming
You'll be a slave to nothing
When you see through my Father's eyes
I'm finding beauty for the first time

Looking through my Father's eyes
(I'm finding beauty for the first time
Looking through my Father's eyes)

His Timing

The Lord's ultimate purpose is to cultivate our hearts and soul to become good soil for His seed. Good soil is about openness to God's visions and ideas. When He speaks, we should listen and always be open to His voice and wondrous ways.

One of the frustrating mysteries to us—and many other impatient leaders—is how slow it seems the Lord moves. He apparently keeps us waiting for opened doors or the resources needed to implement His visions and plans. Sometimes, the waiting involves other people, problems, lack of faith, or fears. But often the issue relates to our misunderstanding of 'time' itself.

In 2 Peter 3:8-9 the Apostle says, *"With the Lord, a day is like a thousand years, and a thousand years are like a day. The Lord is not slow in keeping His promise, as some understand slowness. He is patient with you, does not want anyone to perish, but wants everyone to come to repentance."* In other words, God's timetable is often slower than we'd like. There are character lessons we need to learn as well as events that must be experienced.

The Lord is involved in all of our lives, whether we know it or not. The stages of the soils teach us to trust God while developing our character and obedience to Him. Most importantly, they prepare us for bigger and better things. The Untold Secret that creates true wealth and legends is rooted in the rich soil of God and the relationship we build with Him. It is only through Him that long-term business success is possible.

The Final Word

The public persona or worldly standard of making money, realizing fame, achieving power, and acquiring toys is not the standard of the One who created us. Here on Earth, the popular performance tracking system is measured by how many zeros are added to your income level, gross sales, or net profit. But when we die, none of us gets to take the money and fame with us. This worldly system is not the system of the One who chose us and loves us.

Instead, God is tracking the depth of your love for Him and the support and encouragement you share with others. That is His measure of our success and His True Wealth and Legacy plan. Matthew 7:13 says, *"Broad is the road that leads to destruction, and many enter through it. But small is the gate and narrow the road that leads to life, and only a few will find it."*

In John's interpretation, 'broad' is the road we call life on earth. It is filled with many choices and opportunities. While pursuing pleasure and worldly gains, our souls are being deceived in the process. But true life is about the eternal journey. It involves becoming increasingly focused on your calling and commitment to the One who created you. He is the One who yearns to greet you in Heaven with, *"Well done, thy faithful servant."*

Here are three keys to success in business life that result in both earthly and eternal rewards in wealth:

1. **Discover your God-given talents, calling, and purpose.** It's your assignment, and if you fail to discover it, you will have lived a life that's less than your God-given purpose. Only God by His Spirit imparts and confirms it to us through the visions of His seeds on your soul.

2. **Persevere through the obstacles and trials, successes and failures to find meaning and purpose in each painful or joyous moment.** This is the *"Secret to the Kingdom"* from Jesus' example of sowing seed and be- coming fruitful though a refinement process.

3. **Watch out for false gods and people who will mislead and deceive you.** The Lord is not leading you to fail but allows you to make mistakes for the greater purpose of character development and to prepare you for your calling.

Everyone fails and makes mistakes, because we are born with a birthright of 'free will' to choose our own way. Some are selfish with wrong motive.

Yet your mistakes can toughen and prepare you for the greater journey to your most meaningful calling—developing you from a caterpillar to butterfly. Chances are you won't move from the hard soil to the good soil in one leap. God knows when we're ready to receive the seed. Occasionally, you'll see the alcoholic who suddenly comes to Christ and stops drinking. But what's more typical? You guessed it! The Lord allows us to be broken, to struggle, and to willingly discard the old self-centered heart. He does this to draw us to a new life in Christ.

"No long-term good comes without a sacrifice."

If you are meant to be a leader, there is a very good chance that your scars and disappointments in life will create a deeper walk with God and provide rich opportunities for you to give back. We learn most from pain and then try to help others avoid the same mistake. It is God's method of training and using those experiences for good. Good overcomes evil and light overcomes darkness.

It takes tough people to be successful in our world. It took guts for the early American settlers to leave the security of home and travel the unknown oceans to a new land. It took a spiritual conviction—beyond human logic—to find a place to worship God in a free land. It took tough people to settle this land and make a better life for themselves and their children. We all live under their legacy. Many of the things the Lord asks His people to do are pioneering.

If you examine the 33 years of Jesus' life, you quickly come to realize that He spent only three years in the ministry, spreading the gospel. So, the other 30 years—90% of His life—He spent in preparation for those three years. We are all in that process until we are gone from this earth. Constantly growing, we are learning how to change and become better at what we called to do.

Do Not Forget the LORD

(Deuteronomy 8) NIV excerpted

Moses who wrote the book of Deuteronomy his covenant and speaking for Lord.

> *8 Be careful to follow every command I am giving you today, so that you may live and increase and may enter and possess the land the Lord promised on oath to your ancestors. 2 Remember how the Lord your God led you all the way in the wilderness these forty years, to humble and test you in order to know what was in your heart, whether or not you would keep his commands. 3 He humbled you, causing you to hunger and then feeding you with manna, which neither you nor your ancestors had known, to teach you that man does not live on bread alone but on every word that comes from the mouth of the Lord. 4 Your clothes did not wear out and your feet did not swell during these forty years. 5 Know then in your heart that as a man disciplines his son, so the Lord your God disciplines you.*

> *6 Observe the commands of the Lord your God, walking in obedience to him and revering him.7 For the Lord your God is bringing you into a good land—a land with brooks, streams, and deep springs gushing out into the valleys and hills; 8 a land with wheat and barley, vines and fig trees, pomegranates, olive oil and honey; 9 a land where bread will not be scarce and you will lack nothing; a land where the rocks are iron and you can dig copper out of the hills.*

> *10 When you have eaten and are satisfied, praise the Lord*

your God for the good land he has given you. 11 Be careful that you do not forget the Lord your God, failing to observe his commands, his laws and his decrees that I am giving you this day. 12 Otherwise, when you eat and are satisfied, when you build fine houses and settle down, 13 and when your herds and flocks grow large and your silver and gold increase and all you have is multiplied, 14 then your heart will become proud and you will forget the Lord your God, who brought you out of Egypt, out of the land of slavery. 15 He led you through the vast and dreadful wilderness, that thirsty and waterless land, with its venomous snakes and scorpions. He brought you water out of hard rock. 16 He gave you manna to eat in the wilderness, something your ancestors had never known, to humble and test you so that in the end it might go well with you. 17 You may say to yourself, "My power and the strength of my hands have produced this wealth for me." 18 But remember the Lord your God, for it is he who gives you the ability to produce wealth, and so confirms his covenant, which he swore to your ancestors, as it is today.

19 If you ever forget the Lord your God and follow other gods and worship and bow down to them, I testify against you today that you will surely be destroyed. 20 Like the nations the Lord destroyed before you, so you will be destroyed for not obeying the Lord your God.

Traits of Effective Entrepreneurs Who Achieve True Wealth

1. Take Charge Leader

2. Vision Orientated Innovator

3. Humble Servant Leader

4. Sees His Mission

5. Addicted to Learning

6. Builds Trust and Teamwork

7. Open Minded Listener

8. Hires Superstars

9. Good Communicator

10. Multi-Tasker

11. Wise Decision Maker

12. Prayer Warrior and student of the Word

13. Good Steward and Accountable

*"God does not call the equipped
but equips the called."*

UNKNOWN

> *Visions are spiritually discerned by leaders*
> *...to others they are foolishness* —1 Corinthians 2:14

Visionaries

"If you are called to be a visionary—
many will call you a pioneer—to blaze a new trail.
Others will warn you that you will gather
the most arrows in your back.
But with your trust in the Lord,
you can be sure your efforts will not be in vain."

CHANGING YOUR LIFE FOREVER

Brig Hart Story

As a kid, Brig had many struggles and left home in his early teens. He longed to have the respect and love of his father. His Dad struggled with alcohol, so he and Brig clashed often. After High School and building a Surf Shop with his brother, he decided to join the Marines for 2 years. The Marines helped him mature. After returning home he struggled with an addiction to drugs. He failed to commit suicide and finally one day sitting with a revolver by his side, he planned to take his life, again. But he received a phone call from a businessman he had just met who wanted to have him come to a meeting to learn about a new business opportunity.

Brig thought he had nothing to lose so he decided to go and at the meeting, another Businessman began to read the Bible--1 Corinthians about Love. Brig, said, "That was beautiful, who wrote that?" The gentleman replied I will introduce you to Him. That day changed his life forever as he surrendered to Christ. He says, "the day before I was headed for a life of misery and going to hell. Now I was heading for a life of peace, and joy beyond my comprehension. And what a ride it's been. I love serving the Lord in business and changing the lives of believers and non-believers forever. He has led me to all the success I have enjoyed."

Even though he has faced many ups and downs (including skin cancer that opened the door to partner with MonaVie), Brig has led thousands to a personal relationship with Jesus Christ. He has his own personal ministry and staff to help people get started in their study and walk with the Lord. It's at Newlifenetwork.org

John Beehner's story

One late night in September of 1980, I arrived at the Day's Inn in Fort Lauderdale from Jacksonville to meet some Bank Executives the next day. I was broken and a nervous wreak fully gripped with fear.

The day before I had seen a devil in my mind who was trying to kill me. Desperate and filled with fear I caught a portion of a TV show that night called *"Good News."* The show was sponsored by local Businessmen and I listened to an Attorney from Toronto being interviewed by Demos Sharkarin (the Founder). The words of the attorney touched me and at that moment I knew that Jesus Christ was alive in the hearts of some men who choose to believe. As I heard the attorney say, *"you know my whole life changed when I stopped living my life for myself and started living it for Him."* It brought me to tears for the first time in many years. The next day at lunch the same men's group who sponsored the show were meeting. I was eager to attend and heard a testimony about how a man's life had been changed dramatically by trusting Jesus Christ. After the lunch I had a 5 hour drive to reach my destination but I had taken the only Bible I ever had. I told my wife Judy that I was going to get serious with God.

So here I was in that hotel room. As I started to settle in I noticed a red covered paperback Bible that seemed so much simplier to read than the King James Version, I had brought. As I glanced through it, I was drawn to the back and a prayer for giving your life to Christ. It seemed like a ray of light. I read it many times and I cried out to the Lord many times that evening.

So I am sharing the same words with you in case you want to take the journey with me and millions of others to be able see through the Father's eyes.

Here is the prayer.

"Lord Jesus, I need You.
I open the door of my life and receive You
as the my Savior and Lord.
Thank you for forgiving my sins.
Take control of the thrones of my life.
Make me the kind of person You want me to be."

The Secret of the Kingdom of God is found in the Parable of the Sower and the Seed. As a point of clarification, my reference is the New International Version (NIV) of the Bible. The words ´Mystery of the Kingdom are used in the King James Version of the Bible and all later King James (KJ)translations. The word mystery is used as a synonym and partner with secret according to Webster's Dictionary. But every other translations of the Bible uses the word secret rather than mystery.

More scriptures of inspiration

1 Corinthians 3:19

Matthew 16: 26

John 15:19

John 15:13

John 8:47

1 Corinthians 2:14

Luke 8:10

Matthew 13:11, Mark 4:11 and again in Luke 8:10

Luke 8:14

Matthew 13:30

James 1:3-8

Matthew 7:16

Galatians 5:22

I Corinthians 13:4

Luke 12:15

James 1:2

Luke 6:10-11

Luke 16:10

2 John 15:4

The Untold Secret Resources
(not already noted)

True Wealth By The Book, John F. Beehner,

Why Not You? Why Not Now? The Brig Hart story

Selected personality interviews and their quotes

Personal radio interviews, **Marketplace Witness show**

WAYRadio 550 AM

Os Hillman **TGIF**, daily devotional

Guideposts Multiple stories

Various **Wikipedia** auto-biographical stories

Original Intent, David Barton, Wall Builders

Pour your heart into it, Story of Starbucks

Great Game of Business by Jack Stack

"NUTS" Southwest Airlines Recipe
Kevin and Jackie Freiberg

ABOUT THE AUTHORS

Brig Hart, As a young man enjoyed the carefree life of a surfer whose youthful excesses frequently put him in trouble with local authorities. After a stint in the Marines, a deal worked out with a judge, Brig and his brother open a surf shop on a shoestring budget.

Then a series of events unfolded that transformed Brig's personal and spiritual life, and his business fortunes. Brig started a marketing company that became one of the largest independent sales and marketing machines in Amway history. Tens of thousands of people attended his events. Famous people challenged the audience from Brig's stage. Inspired to never give up, many of Brig's team became wealthy beyond their wildest dreams.

A few years, after closing that chapter of his life, Brig discovered he had skin cancer. On a quest to find healing, he discovered a little known fruit and berry company in Utah named Mona Vie. As he used the product to help his body heal, he became convinced it could help anyone. So he invested in MonaVie and helped create a foundation for what became one of the largest organizations in direct sales history. They recruited over 1 million distributors and that produced 1 Billion in sales in it first 3 years in business.

Brig and Lita Hart newest venture is the USA Association to help *"take back the USA"*...from liberal leaning and get back to faith, family and free enterprise. Many believe that Brig is a master of faith and inspiration who has and continues to inspire everyone he meets.

John Beehner, is an author, entrepreneur, and business coach. He is Founder and CEO of Wise Counsel, an ongoing roundtable learning process for entrepreneurs of faith. He has personally worked with over hundreds of business owners for more than 30 years. He has seen and studied the strategies and tools that companies use through the cycles of success and failure. John lays a solid foundation in his books by comparing the world's view of success with that of America's founding fathers who sought the Bible for their principles and values. Through real-life stories and illustrations, John drives his point home in inspirational ways.

In 1981, John founded an organization formerly known as TEC in Florida and rapidly built the business to over 300 clients with 20 staff people help small to midsize grow an average 20% a year. They focused on the strategies that drive business success with outside experts, coaching and using the talents and gifts of peer CEOs in sharing their advise, wisdom and personal experiences. He personally worked with two clients who had grown from $2 million to $2 billion in 15 years. Both received the coveted Horatio Alger Award given to Distinguished Americans who overcome adversity in achieving excellence.

John is author of *"True Wealth By the Book"* and the popular video series *"Genesis: the Business Workshop."* These resources provide insights on how to build their business on a solid foundation of Biblical and business values. John's second book is entitled *"The Freedom Revolution... Rocking our World. The inspiring story of how freedom and the church are transforming nations."* He also hosts his own local radio show known as *"Marketplace Witness"* were he interviews business and ministry leaders to learn from their life story.

7156698R00110

Made in the USA
San Bernardino, CA
26 December 2013